Santa Clara SAGAS

by AUSTEN D. WARBURTON

With a Foreword by PAUL LOCATELLI, S.J.
President of Santa Clara University

Edited by MARY JO IGNOFFO

CALIFORNIA HISTORY CENTER & FOUNDATION
CUPERTINO, CALIFORNIA
LOCAL HISTORY STUDIES VOLUME 36

Copyright © by California History Center Foundation, 1996. All rights reserved, including the right of reproduction in any form. Published by the California History Center & Foundation, De Anza College, 21250 Stevens Creek Blvd., Cupertino, California 95014. N. Kathleen Peregrin, director.

Library of Congress Cataloging-in-Publication Data

Warburton, Austen D., 1917–1995.
    Santa Clara sagas/by Austen D. Warburton; edited by Mary Jo Ignoffo.
    108 p. 27.9x21.6 cm. — (Local History studies; v. 36)
    Includes index.
    ISBN 0-935089-20-9 (hard cover).
    ISBN 0-935089-19-5 (soft cover).
    1. Santa Clara (Calif.)—History. 2. Santa Clara (Calif.)—Biography. 3. Santa Clara (Calif.)—Civilization. I. Ignoffo, Mary Jo. II. Title. III. Series.
F869.S47W37 1996
979.4'73—dc20

96-31645
CIP

FRONT COVER:
Main Street, Santa Clara, California, circa 1900. Fatjo & Somavia Real Estate and Insurance office is on the left edge next to the saddlery. The Post Office is on the far right with Alderman's Cigar and Stationery Store next to it. Santa Clara Valley Bank is the prominent building with awnings at the corner of Main and Franklin streets. Courtesy the Austen Warburton Collection.

BACK COVER:
Austen Den Warburton, 1917–1995
Portrait of Austen Warburton by Bob Gerbracht on display at the Triton Museum of Art, Santa Clara, California. Print courtesy of Joan Rogers.

TITLE PAGE:
Stage coach in Santa Clara circa 1880s. Courtesy Santa Clara University Archives.

CONTENTS

FOREWORD

Austen Warburton, author of Santa Clara Sagas, died on May 2, 1995 and a memorial service was held three days later at Mission Santa Clara de Asís. At the memorial service, the following precis of the homily drawn from reflections by his family and friends, was delivered by Paul Locatelli, S.J., President of Santa Clara University.

AUSTEN WARBURTON: A FRIEND FOR ALL SEASONS

Austen Warburton was a friend whom we all will miss. His wonderfully human touch will leave an emptiness in our hearts. Yet, our troubled hearts [John 14:1-6] are also mingled with gratitude to God and peace in our hearts [Col. 3:12-17].

Gratitude comes now from the fact of thanking God for the gift of life, for the gift of someone who was a genuine friend and teacher of life, and for revealing something of God's presence and power in our community. Austen loved throughout a long life, always learning through God's grace to serve others. In a quiet and unassuming way, he helped people of all walks of life.

Austen was like all of us, not perfect. We are still part of the old earth where love remains a daily task, yet visible in the faces of many. As Christians, we see God fully shining in the human face of Jesus. And it is equally true that we see a glimmer of God in the faces of all believers who spread peace and good will, and at this moment in the features of Austen's face.

Peace will come when we understand that we also will one day join Austen in God's house with its many dwelling places—and when we grasp how he was a man of deep faith, hope and love.

What I am about to try is virtually impossible: to capture the many faces of love visible in Austen's life. A few stories by his family, colleagues and friends will give us a glimpse of his virtues that inspire us to call him *a friend for all seasons.*

A MAN OF FAITH: Austen had faith in God and faith in people. Most clearly reflecting his faith in people have been the many stories of his public service. These stories have often been published in the press and recounted in the city square. What is not as well chronicled is his constant pattern of generously giving of himself to the young and elderly, rich and poor, marginated and friends. All were equally important to Austen. This is faith.

Some stories will testify to his faith:

He was always there for each of us whenever we needed him. He took the time to listen, to care and to be our friend. (niece)

No matter how busy his schedule, there was always time for others. (friend)

When he became ill, his concern was for those around him rather than himself. He was truly amazed and surprised at the outpouring of support for him. At the same time he was concerned about those saddened by his disease. He didn't want them feeling bad for him—this (the cancer) was just a part of life. (friend)

When he was no longer able to come to the office we came to him. He would always want to know what was going on at the office and many times asked me if "I was taking care of thing." He was more concerned about his "office family" and clients and how they were doing than his own disease. (colleague)

About five years ago we were planning a family outing to Great America. Mr. Warburton's secretary at the time told us we should tell him because he might be able to get us a good deal on admission. When we told him of our plans, expecting at most a coupon or something, he said "ok, how about I meet you there on Saturday around 10 o'clock and I'll get you in free." Sure enough, on Saturday at 10 o'clock he showed up and gave us all free admission tickets. His taking time . . . . truly amazed me. (friend)

A Jesuit from Santa Clara had a long conversation with Austen about his sickness. Austen hoped that God would permit him to return to good health and said he was praying for a miracle because he believed he had experienced something like that earlier in life.

When he was much younger, Austen discovered he had cancer. His doctors determined that there was nothing they could do. With no other recourse, Austen asked God for a miracle. And it was his deep belief that his prayer was answered. With tears in his eyes, he explained how he had been cured and what a profound experience recovery had been for him.

Moved by the account, the Jesuit said: "Austen, what do you think God was telling you by this?" Looking the priest directly in the eye he said, "What was God telling me? Get off your butt!" (An atypical statement from the usually eloquent and gentlemanly Austen).

And Austen did just that. He came to appreciate life much more than ever before and was determined to make the best use of the time and life God gave him. With a much deeper faith from that experience, he became even more determined to be generous with others.

A MAN OF HOPE: Austen was a man of hope. His orientation of spirit and heart was able to look beyond the immediacy of the moment into the mystery and goodness of life. His yearning to teach especially the young; his willingness to invest his life in helping others; his desire to do something because it is good; his quest for making life and our community better are all signs of hope.

Many stories reveal to us this man of hope:

I best remember his vast knowledge about plants, trees, rocks—the things of the world. He had a great interest in everything, knew its name and often how it got its name, and something of its history or importance. (niece)

By teaching us about our past, our ancestry, he has given us an irreplaceable gift to pass on to our children and theirs. Through his example we have learned so many things: a love and respect for nature, compassion for others, and a sense of community spirit and responsibility. His optimism in all things was infectious. And in the end, his final lesson to us was one of courage. (grandniece)

If great-great nieces Beth or Amy asked him to speak at their school, with great enthusiasm he would agree. And when we mentioned 4th grade mission reports were coming up—look out!—pack up the car—Santa Barbara here we come, with the best California tour guide there is. (grandniece)

It often seemed we were learning together, but that was simply his own subtle, yet clever, way of imparting his vast knowledge to me (and to all others who sought his counsel). . . . He will remain a tremendous presence in my life, and his words of wisdom shall stay with me for a very long time. (colleague)

As teacher he also gave hope to his colleagues. His professional colleagues provided a list of "We Remember Austen Warburton" who:

loved hiking and the mountains, or counting stars at his ranch.

giving talks to Russian and Polish exchange students—and gifts of jeans and a trip to Safeway for the experience.

always did his Christmas shopping on the last day.

mid-way through a meal would ask "What's for dessert?" and when the tray of desserts arrived, his eyes would widen and his face gleam!

used to teach pleading and practice without a text-book.

A MAN OF LOVE: Austen showed us love. He gave of himself making his love visible in his words and deeds. The vignettes revealing his faith and hope and the many more untold stories reveal his deep and abiding love for people.

His colleagues also saw his love when:

he always bought lunch.

he would go grocery shopping for his elderly clients.

every Saturday morning he ran a community program for at least 30 years counseling juveniles.

he lived by the Bible story of the widow's mite.

he showed appreciation for each and every employee.

Joan Rogers, Austen's niece, received a condolence letter from the White House.

Dear Joan:

I was sorry to learn of your uncle's death. Austen Warburton was a remarkable man who gave much to Santa Clara and to our nation.

From his work on the Santa Clara City Council and throughout his distinguished career, Austen's integrity, wisdom, and energy won him the profound respect of his friends and colleagues. His unflagging commitment to public service and to the advancement of the arts sets an example to which we can all aspire. He will long be remembered by all those whose lives he enriched.

Hillary and I offer our deepest sympathy to you and your family, and we will keep you in our prayers.

Sincerely,
Bill Clinton

For Austen, ordinary people were just as important as those in high places. The letter from Bill Clinton would have meant a great deal to him, but I suspect a poem by a young friend of Austen's would have touched his heart more profoundly.

The large gathering to celebrate Austen's life is also testimony to the fact that Austen lived the virtues of faith, hope and love. His life mirrored Christ's life—to have faith in life, to show us that love is kind and patient, to love children and the elderly, to give hope to others often the most fragile, to show mercy, to teach peace and generosity, to forgive others and be forgiven, to have the courage to do what is just and good rather than convenient.

Because Austen was a man for all seasons who always gave witness to God's presence and love in this world, we now have confidence that he is at peace in the new heaven. Our faith is not one of doubt, but as William Wordsworth put it: "the faith that looks through death." We cannot always explain that faith, yet it turns our troubled hearts into hearts at peace.

Our hope says he is sharing in the fullness of life face-to-face with God. And, our love turns to great gratitude for God having given him to us, and for a glimpse of Christ through him.

And, in the end, we can say with the Jesuit poet Gerard Manley Hopkins:

Acts in God's eye what in God's eye he is—Christ
For Christ plays in ten thousand places,
Lovely in limbs, and lovely in eyes not his
To the Father through the features of men's faces.

And through the features of Austen's face.

PAUL LOCATELLI, S.J.
Mission Church at
Santa Clara University
May 5, 1995

EDITOR'S INTRODUCTION

The late Austen Warburton, attorney, philanthropist, patron of the arts and history buff, wrote a series of stories about Santa Clara families which appeared in the *Santa Clara American* during the 1970s and 1980s. Based on his long-term service as trustee to the California History Center & Foundation, he made arrangements for some of the articles to be compiled and published as one of its local history series. The result is Local History Studies Volume 36, *Santa Clara Sagas*, which recounts memories and experiences of some families about their town and how they came to live there.

Warburton's essays reveal as much about himself as they do about the families. Clearly he displays a passion for family history, whether his own or others', as he details multi-generation genealogies. In addition, his personal work ethic is emphasized: the notion that hard work pays handsome dividends. Warburton also affirms a serious commitment to community service, and especially admires those who expend great energy for the community over and above their chosen professions. He discusses bartenders and shopkeepers who served on city council, and mothers and cannery workers who organized church or civic benefits.

Warburton was clearly intrigued by stories about pioneers. Voyages over oceans and treks across continents captured his imagination and he communicates details of those journeys. Whether he is describing 49ers rushing to California to stake their claims or early 20th-century Spanish immigrants fleeing poverty, his admiration for the gutsy wherewithal of the pioneer is palpable. And he seems equally impressed by pioneering women as men.

Warburton also displays an empathy for children and the lasting effect that childhood experiences impart. In one of the more poignant stories, Jennie (Pogue) Jepson was sent away from her Hawaiian home by her parents at age four to be raised by a maiden aunt in Santa Clara. "Many nights in Santa Clara she would awaken from a dream thinking that her parents were at the front door ringing the bell. She would run down the flight of stairs but finding no one there, would climb back up and cry herself to sleep." Warburton was clearly touched by the story.

On the lighter side, there is evidence of the author's sense of romance. In many cases he took great pains to discover how married couples first met and uses phrases like "romance blossomed" or "love-at-first-sight." We are given an insight into courtship and marriage in the small town, and how some people chose their spouses.

This collection is important as a way to examine major historical events from a local perspective. Whether the mission era or the gold rush, the Depression or a world war, each comes into focus from a new angle when its impact on an individual or family is recounted. What at first glance may appear anecdotal can reveal a glimpse of Santa Clara of another time. Santa Clarans' attitudes toward labor, education, child-rearing, courtship and marriage, alcohol consumption, or local politics are suddenly illuminated. *Santa Clara Sagas* can also serve as a steppingstone to further histor-ical research of many of these broader topics.

Santa Clara Sagas has been divided into chapters about religion, commerce, politics, immigration, law and culture. This collection does not attempt to be an exhaustive history of the city of Santa Clara and so, for example, the religion chapter tells but one story, not all religious activity in the town. Likewise, the immigration chapter focuses on early 20th-century Spaniards, not the numerous other immigrant groups. Family stories have been clustered around the topic which best relates to them. With some exceptions which are noted, the photographs were chosen from the author's collection which he compiled with help from the families over a number of years. Within the chapters, some short arti-cles appear in shaded boxes which have been added by the editor to complement and provide background for the stories. As a point of clarification, all references to the college in Santa Clara, which for a long time was called Santa Clara College, then the University of Santa Clara, have been changed to Santa Clara University, the current name of the school.

These stories were written by a man who was devoted to his community, who worked with its citizens and loved its history. His personal relationship with most of the families in this collection allowed an entree into some lives that may not have otherwise been recorded. By the same token, perhaps precisely because of his very personal involvement, Mr. Warburton is not critical of events or decisions in Santa Clara's past. He chose to emphasize the positive and leave critical com-mentaries to others.

I am grateful to a number of people for their help with this publication. The staff and the board of trustees of the California History Center and Joan Rogers, Mr. Warburton's niece, entrusted this project to me. Julia O'Keefe, archivist at Santa Clara University and Bea Lichtenstein of the Santa Clara Arts and Historical Consortium helped locate some photographs, and Sam Winklebleck previewed the finalized text. To each, and to my family, thank you.

Although I met Mr. Warburton only a few times, working with his text has allowed me to get to know a little more about him. The values he imparts through his essays can inspire a whole new generation to cherish their families, take pride in their work, and in some way, serve the community. I appreciate having had the opportunity to edit *Santa Clara Sagas*.

MARY JO IGNOFFO
Editor
March 1996

INTRODUCTION

Before the City of Santa Clara was established, the area was a relatively flat verdant plain studded with large valley oak trees and crossed by streams later named the Guadalupe, San Tomás Aquino, and Calabasas Creeks whose banks were lined with willow, sycamore, and bay trees. The valley lies between the Mt. Hamilton range on the east, rising to over 4,000 feet in elevation, and the redwood forested Santa Cruz mountains on the west, rising to an elevation of about 2,000 feet. The mountains and valley were home to a multitude of wildlife and great herds of deer and elk roamed freely where coyote, bobcat and mountain lions sought their prey. The streams abounded with fish, and the San Francisco Bay and its estuaries attracted great flocks of water fowl which nested in reeds and tules growing profusely along the banks and shore.

Perhaps as long as 10,000 years ago the first human inhabitants made their way into the area that is now Santa Clara. The equitable climate and ample food and water supplies allowed families to form small villages, especially along the streams and near the bay. For thousands of years they fished and hunted and gathered nuts and grain.

When the first Europeans entered the area in 1769, they called the Indians *Los Costanos* or "the coastal people." It was the presence of many of these natives that persuaded Franciscan missionaries under the direction of Father Junípero Serra to establish a mission named for Saint Clare of Assisi along the banks of the Guadalupe River on January 12, 1777. The nearby Indian village of wickiups made of tules was called "Thamien" by the natives. The first mission was destroyed by flooding from the Guadalupe River soon after it was constructed. Franciscans Tomás de la Peña and José Antonio Murguía, with Indian help, constructed a new church on higher ground near what is now the main entrance to Santa Clara University. Father Junípero Serra himself participated in the laying of the cornerstone in 1781 and returned in May of 1784 for the dedication of the chapel, which he described as being the loveliest in California. The building, however, was damaged by a series of earthquakes and was replaced in 1822 on what is now the campus of Santa Clara University. Hundreds of Indians lived at this and other California missions and were baptized and taught the Spanish way of life by the padres.

A pueblo was established on the opposite side of the Guadalupe River, a few miles upstream from the mission. San José dates from November 29, 1777, and had as its first residents Spaniards to whom plots of land were given for agricultural purposes. There was no church in San José so a road was built, The Alameda, for the Spaniards to go for Mass at Santa Clara. Thus the Spanish priests and supporting *soldados* became the first non-native residents of Santa Clara.

With Mexican independence from Spain in 1821, California became a province of that new republic. During the Mexican regime new faces from other lands began to appear in California, some visiting Santa Clara and later taking up residence there. With the conclusion of the United States' war with Mexico and the Treaty of Guadalupe Hidalgo in 1848, California was ceded by Mexico to the United States and was admitted to the Union on September 9, 1850. Under Spain and Mexico, Monterey had been the capital and it was in that city that the Constitution for the new state was first prepared. Upon admission to the Union the capital was transferred to San José. Legislators were disenchanted with the facilities in San José, and the capital was moved to Vallejo, then to Benicia, and ultimately to Sacramento. Nevertheless, there was a steady influx of people into the Santa Clara Valley and a number of them settled in Santa Clara.

Mission lands had been secularized under the Mexican Government and large grants of land given to various people including some Indians. One grant was given to an Indian known as Yñigo. Part of his holdings later became Moffett Field. Yñigo had been converted at the mission.

José Sadoc Alemany, the Catholic bishop of San Francisco, recognized the need for higher education in California and sent a contingent of Italian Jesuits under the leadership of Father John Nobili to take over the old mission at Santa Clara in order to establish a college. In 1851, Nobili founded what has now become Santa Clara University, and the administration continued under a succession of Jesuit Fathers educating not only local students but many who have come from the far corners of the world to enjoy the educational opportunity.

The City of Santa Clara was incorporated on July 5, 1852. The core of the community was laid out with streets running basically north and south and east and west, named for a number of American heroes and political figures such as Washington, Lincoln, Jefferson, Jackson, Benton, Fremont, Madison and Harrison.

I have endeavored to explore the stories of some of the people who over the years have built the City of Santa Clara. Although they have come from many places over many years, there is an inspiring similarity to their stories. We shall hear of people in faraway lands who yearned for opportunity in a new world. Often at great risk and sacrifice they came, some by sea and some by land. Although financial resources were limited, they were willing to work and worked hard. They raised families. They built churches and schools. They educated their children, they saved money, acquired properties, built homes and prospered. Horatio Alger could have based his stories on the lives of so many of these early Santa Clarans!

It has been my good fortune to have lived and worked with many of these families and to have had the opportunity to obtain much information concerning them. They have been gracious in making their stories available to all of us and providing pictures and other memorabilia which are included with this historic account.

I also want to extend my thanks to Dr. James Williams of the California History Center at De Anza College in Cupertino, California and to other members of the center and to Sam Winklebleck who have so kindly helped me in the preparation and organization of the material being presented in this book.

—A.D.W.
1994

Chapter One

RELIGION

Mission Santa Clara and Junípero Serra

Junípero Serra, baptized Miguel José Serra on the day he was born, November 24, 1713, in the village of Petra on the Island of Mallorca, Spain, was one of the first persons to contribute to the founding of Santa Clara. It was by his authority that Mission Santa Clara was established on January 12, 1777. Today his name is found on highways, schools and religious organizations.

Serra's parents, Antonio Serra and Margarita Ferrer, were married in 1707 in St. Peter's church in Petra. They had five children, three of whom died in infancy. Miguel José and his sister, Juana Maria, were raised on a farm in the small community. Eventually, Juana Maria married Miguel Ribot y Botellas, and one of her children became a Franciscan mathematician, architect, and author, Fray Miguel de Petra, with whom Junípero Serra conducted correspondence in later years.

Miguel José's parents were very devout and introduced him to the Franciscans who were well established in the area. They sent the boy to Palma, the capital, to be educated and he was inspired to become a Franciscan. Initially he was turned down because he was too young and too small, but eventually he did enter the order at the age of 16, on September 14, 1730. He was a studious and pious young man who was particularly interested in the lives of the saints.

The following year, on September 15, 1731, Serra took his first vows as a Franciscan, assuming the name "Junípero" from Brother Juniper, a simple, humble, charitable man, who was a companion of St. Francis of Assisi. Serra had read that St. Francis once said of Juniper, "Would to God, my brethren, that I had a great forest of such junipers." Six years later, Serra was ordained a priest. He studied philosophy and theology and earned the degree of Doctor of Sacred Theology. Then he was elected professor of philosophy for the Friary. One of his students, Francisco Palóu, also entered the Franciscan order and became Serra's close friend and companion. Palóu would later chronicle Serra's life.

The two friars wanted to become missionaries to the Indians of the Americas, and they obtained permission to go to Mexico where the Franciscans ran the College of San Fernando near Mexico City. They joined a group of missionaries sailing from Cadiz, Spain, to Vera Cruz, Mexico, a trip that took 99 days. Toward the latter part of the voyage, supplies became desperately short.

En route from Vera Cruz to the College of San Fernando, a journey on foot and by pack mule, Serra was bitten by insects and his leg became irritated and swollen, leading to a condition which was painful and burdensome to him the rest of his life. Serra and Palóu arrived at the college on January 1, 1750, and after five months, Serra learned that missionaries were needed to go to the Sierra Gorda area of northern Mexico where the Pame Indians lived. He volunteered and was made president of the five missions of the area, travelling to them on foot and devoting the next eight years of his life to Christianizing the Indians and teaching them how to live as Spaniards: the men how to farm and construct buildings, and the women how to sew and weave. As the missions flourished, Serra's reputation for missionary work spread.

The expulsion of the Jesuits from Mexico in 1767 caused Viceroy de Croix to transfer the Jesuit missions in Baja California to the Franciscans of the College of San Fernando. Serra was named president of the 16 Franciscan missionaries who replaced the Jesuits in the region. Serra's group, after some delays, boarded the packet boat *La Concepcion* at San Blas and sailed to Loreto, arriving on Good Friday in 1768.

Shortly thereafter, Visitador General Don José de Gálvez visited the Baja missions to confer with Serra about a northward colonization as part of a general Spanish program to protect the wealth of the empire from encroachments by England, France, and Russia. Gálvez's proposal involved planting settlements in Alta California, and he and Serra agreed that three missions should be established in Alta California: one at San Diego, one at Monterey, and the other, to be called San Buenaventura, in between.

The expedition was to proceed from Baja California by both sea and land. The flagship of the expedition, *San Carlos*, packed with supplies to establish the missions, including religious artifacts, farm implements, and seeds, departed La Paz on January 9, 1969, after a grand exhortation by the Visitador General. Captain Vicente Vila commanded the ship, accompanied by Lieutenant Pedro Fages, 25 soldiers, and military engineer, Miguel Costansó. The two other

Mission Santa Clara's cornerstone, set in 1781 and accidentally rediscovered by a local man in 1911. Currently it is on display at de Saisset Museum, Santa Clara University. Photo by Austen Warburton, 1987.

ships sailed within a month.

Gaspar de Portolá was appointed governor of California and commander of the entire expedition and was assisted by Captain Fernando de Rivera y Moncada. They divided the land expedition into two units, Rivera leading the first and Portolá the second, and gathered in an area known as Velicatá. Food for the trip included dried and salted meat, seeds, flour, hard tack, and 200 head of cattle. With Father Crespí as diarist, the first unit departed March 24, 1769, arriving at San Diego on May 14 to find two of the three ships already there.

The second unit of the expedition included Serra and Portolá. Because Serra's leg was swollen and painful, Portolá did not think it advisable for Serra to attempt the journey. Serra, however, insisted on going and, hearing that muleteer Juan Antonio Coronel had some knowledge of veterinary medicine, requested that the same remedy for an animal wound be applied to him. Coronel took some tallow and herbs, fried the mixture into a poultice, and applied it to Serra's leg. According to Palóu, Serra slept well that night and was able to move forward the next day with Portolá and the expedition.

Portolá's and Serra's group arrived at San Diego on July 1 to find the entire party exhausted and those who had come by sea stricken with scurvy. Nevertheless, within two weeks Portolá, Rivera, Costanso, Father Crespí, and others pressed northward to find the port of Monterey. Serra stayed behind to care for the sick, and on July 16, he founded Mission San Diego de Alcalá, the first of the missions of Alta California.

Portolá's expedition proceeded northerly on a route

Painting of Fray Junípero Serra which longtime Carmel Mission curator Harry Downie came upon in 1956 in Zacatecas, Mexico.

that would become *El Camino Real*, "the King's Highway." Finding the way impassable in the area of Big Sur, they crossed the coastal range and entered the Salinas Valley. When they reached Monterey Bay from the valley, the party believed they were in the right location, but they failed to recognize it, for they could see nothing of the fine harbor praised in 1603 by the explorer Vizcaíno. Portolá led his men northward, along the coast, finding and naming the San Lorenzo River. They were the first Europeans to report seeing redwood trees. While camped near Montara, Sergeant José Ortega led a scouting party ahead and discovered what is now known as San Francisco Bay. In an unsuccessful attempt to pass around the bay, Ortega became the first European to enter what are now the city limits

of Santa Clara. Portolá's expedition returned to San Diego to find that a group of local Indians had attacked Serra and the others who stayed behind. The attackers had been driven off, but one of the priests had been shot in the hand with an arrow. Palóu wrote later that in 1775, six years after the incident, another attack was made against the mission by the same Indian group. Eventually an Indian was captured and identified as the leader of the group. Serra sought the Indian's repentence, to baptize him and bring him into the mission fold, but the Indian refused and, according to Palóu, remained imprisoned and committed suicide several years later.

Portolá returned to Monterey in 1770 and established a presidio. Serra founded Mission San Carlos Borromeo there but relocated it the next year to a site overlooking the Carmel River. The next several years were arduous ones. Serra feuded with Lieutenant Pedro Fages, who had been appointed governor after Portolá's job was done and who repeatedly vetoed Serra's plans for new missions.

By 1775, however, Fages had been replaced by Fernando de Rivera, and support from Mexico was stronger. In September 1776, Rivera received a letter from Viceroy Bucareli in which he indicated he believed two missions had been established near the bay of San Francisco. Rivera, who had obstructed these plans for some time, went to Monterey to learn that the Mission San Francisco de Asís (popularly known as Mission Dolores) had indeed been established by Serra. In order to found the second mission in the area, Father Tomas de la Peña was assigned to survey the territory.

Rivera and de la Peña arrived in today's Santa Clara Valley, discovering a broad plain much like one in southern California named in honor of San Bernardino. They travelled across it and discovered a river containing a good flow of water running to the bay of San Francisco. They also found springs of running water that could be used to irrigate the land. There

Post card of a re-creation of the library at Mission San Carlos Borromeo (Carmel), the first library in California. Its first books were brought by Fray Junípero Serra and by 1820 it had over 2,000 volumes. Courtesy Austen Warburton Collection.

were Indian villages, many large oaks, and the place seemed quite fitting for a mission. Fathers José Murguía and de la Peña brought supplies to the new mission site. An altar was established under a shelter and Father de la Peña said the first mass on January 12, 1777, marking the founding of the Mission Santa Clara de Asís. Father Palóu later commented that this mission probably occupied the best place in all of Alta California, since it was situated on a vast plain which was over 90 miles long and from nine to 15 miles wide. He wrote:

It has good soil for agriculture and abundant harvests of wheat and corn and every kind of vegetable are produced. These are sufficient not only to maintain the neophytes, but also to present to the pagans to attract them to the bosom of the Holy Church, and to provide for soldiers of presidios, who exchange for the produce clothing to cover the neophytes. It has an abundance of water, obtained from the river of Nuestra Senora de Guadalupe, which is about a quarter of a league distant from the houses of the mission. In this river good trout are caught in summer. I have seen one that weighed four pounds; I eat of it, and it tasted like salmon trout, quite delicious. Besides the water from the river, the plain has a number of springs, the waters of which run through aqueducts as irrigation for plantings.

Unfortunately, in January 1779 heavy rains caused the Guadalupe River to flood and only quick work by

Post card of a re-creation of Fray Junípero Serra's bedroom at Mission San Carlos Borromeo (Carmel). He died in his room in 1784. Courtesy Austen Warburton Collection.

the padres, soldiers, and Indians saved the church vessels and the household utensils. Serra, writing of this problem to the Father Guardian Rafael Verger in Mexico City said, "Father Peña fled together with his group of Christians; he now resides at a distance of about a half a league, in the place called El Roblar. Father Murguía, so as not abandon the provisions, took refuge nearby and now lives on some higher ground that looked more promising." Father Serra further commented on the failure of the citizens in the nearby pueblo of San José to help the padres:

Neither their [the padres] *good deeds in serving the settlers all the year round, nor their having put up with the annoyance of having their pueblo established close by—contrary to the law, and the governor admits that this is so—nor the request they made in writing to the said governor were of any avail in securing the addition of even one or two sol-*

diers to the six alloted to the mission. If in the meantime there should be anyone sick, they [the Pobladores of San Jose] will most certainly call on the fathers to hear their confessions and assist them.

Serra visited Santa Clara, performed several baptisms, and was able to learn details concerning the moving of the mission. A log church was built at a temporary site and was called the Mission Santa Clara de Thamien (in the laurelwood), and Serra also performed baptisms and confirmations there. While Serra was there a cornerstone was prepared for the permanent mission which was to be built near today's entrance to Santa Clara University. In the first Book of Baptisms, Father Junípero Serra, president of the missions, signed the entry which read:

on the 19th day of November in the Year of Our Lord 1781, in this mission of our Seraphic Mother, Santa Clara of Thamien, after having, on the afternoon of the preceeding day, erected in this place the standard of the holy cross, we have the blessing and laying of the cornerstone of the temple or church, which was commenced on said day as a house of our great God and Lord, with the title of the glorious Santa Clara of Assisi, Virgin Abbess and First Mother of her most celebrated order.

In the cavity of the cornerstone there were enclosed a cross, images, and several coins. In 1911, John Vierra of Santa Clara discovered the cornerstone while digging a ditch in the street. Today the cornerstone and its contents are on display at de Saisset Museum at Santa Clara University.

The building of the church proceeded under the guidance of Father Murguía, who was noted for his architectural skills in the Sierra Gorda mission area of Mexico. The structure was completed and a dedication was planned for mid-May 1784. On Sunday, May 2, Serra was present, and sang the high mass, and with the

Mission San Carlos Borromeo (Carmel), circa 1900. Photograph by Hallett-Taylor Company.

assistance of Murguía and de la Peña, administered confirmation to 143 children, seventy-six of whom were Indians, while the others were children of Spanish and Mexican soldiers and pueblo pioneers from San José. The first child confirmed was a nine-year-old boy, Anselmo de Jesus, who was from the *Rancheria de Santa Aqueda*. His *padrino* (sponsor) was none other than Don Pedro Fages, Lieutenant Colonel and Governor of California. Another was Joseph Hermenegildo Vasquez (spelled Basquez in the mission records), who was listed as the son of Tibursio Vasquez

and Maria Bojorquez, settlers of the Pueblo de San José de Guadalupe. His *padrino* was a soldier, Phelipe Santiago Tapia.

The following day, May 3, Father Serra confirmed an additional 27 children. According to the record entered by de la Peña, when Serra heard that a number of Indians bringing their children for confirmation had arrived late, he held a special evening service "with festive ringing of the bells." He confirmed another 32 children, beginning with Raphael Augustin, a 10-year-old boy from the *Rancheria de San Carlos* whose *padrino*

Franciscan missionaries in the New World.

The College of San Fernando did not offer traditional college training. Missionary candidates arriving from Spain had already completed theological and academic training. Indeed, Serra held a doctoral degree. Instead, San Fernando's goal was intensive training for men to undergo the rigors of living a spartan life, far from any trappings of their European culture. The training included a meatless, meager diet and little sleep. Many candidates practiced self-flagellation or burning flesh as a penitential and mystical religious experience. Junípero Serra spent five months in training at the college, then was sent to administer missions of the Sierra Gorda region of Mexico.

Three groups of missions were administered by the College of San Fernando: those of the Sierra Gorda, Baja California and Alta California. By 1833 however, the missions of Alta California were administered by Mexican-born Franciscans of the College of Zacatecas: those Spanish-born padres of the College of San Fernando were expelled from Alta California.

During Mexico's mid-19th-century War of the Reform, much of the college and church was ransacked. In 1908, the College of San Fernando was formally abolished, and the buildings, save the church, were razed in 1935. Today the Church of San Fernando is Mexico City's second largest church, after the Cathedral.

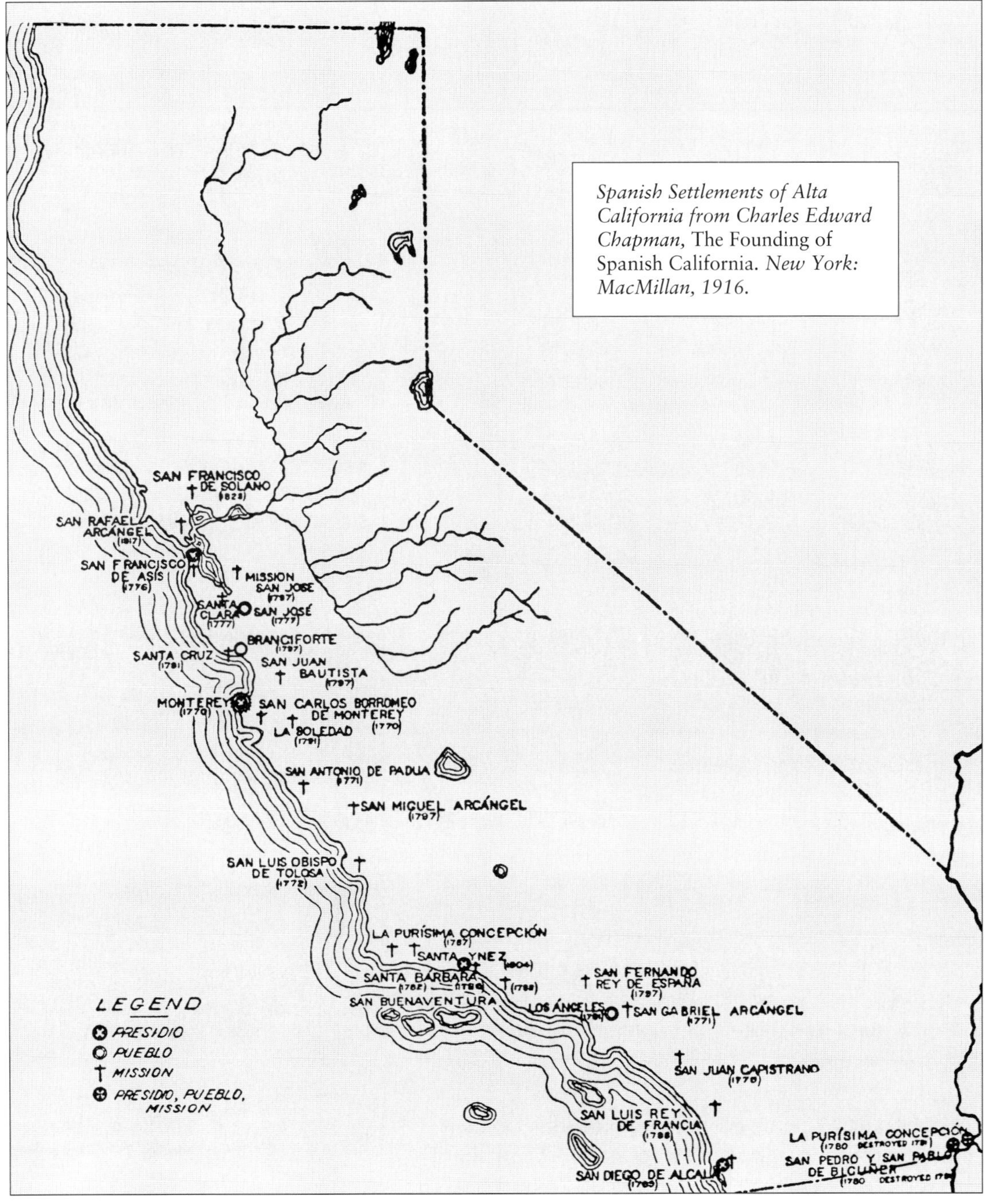

Spanish Settlements of Alta California from Charles Edward Chapman, The Founding of Spanish California. *New York: MacMillan, 1916.*

was soldier Don Gabriel Moraga.

The next day, the aging Serra went to San Francisco for confirmations at Mission Dolores. Meanwhile, Father José Murguía was seriously ill, and Palóu, his old friend and companion of years in Sierra Gorda, hastened from San Francisco to Santa Clara. Although Serra planned to attend the dedication of Murguía's new church at Santa Clara on May 16, Palóu tells us that Serra's involvement with confirmations in San Francisco prevented him from returning to Santa Clara before Murguía's death.

When Serra had finished confirmations at San Francisco, he went to Santa Clara with Governor Fages who had been invited to the dedication of the church. The Governor's party arrived in Santa Clara on the morning of May 15. A solemn blessing was prayed in the afternoon with the entire village together with troops and inhabitants of the Pueblo of San José present.

With acolytes bearing the cross, candles, and other necessary items, the key to the church "was handed to Don Pedro Fages, Lieutenant-Colonel of the Royal Army and Military and Civil Governor of both Californias, as Patron of the ceremony, an office which he gladly accepted." With him was the lieutenant-commandant of the Royal Presidio of St. Francis, Don José Joaquin Moraga. "All arranged in order, we proceeded to the main door of the church, which was locked and we began the blessing of the church. Everything was conducted according to the prescriptions of the Roman ritual. The celebration was carried on amid the ringing of bells, salutes from the muskets of the soldiers and with the fireworks of the mission."

Serra believed Mission Santa Clara was the most beautiful of the churches yet built in California. Father de la Peña described it:

The church walls are one vara and a half thick [a vara is approximately one yard] *of adobe, on stone foundations, supported by buttresses one vara thick.*

Its dimensions inside are eight varas high, forty and one half long, and nine varas wide. The sacristy, which is in the rear of the chancel, has the same height and thickness of the walls of the church; its length is equal to the width of the church, and its width is six varas. A portico measuring five varas extends, as regards the roof, along the entire length of the building. In the church and sacristy there is a flat ceiling of wooden beams on brackets with the planking of the wood of alerche, commonly called redwood. Above this flat ceiling there is a pavement of adobe flags, and above all there is a slanting roof well adapted for drainage. The brackets extend beyond the walls as also the thatch of the roof, to protect the walls from the rains, which are very abundant. The main door and the cloister door, each having two leaves, are made of cedar and redwood, respectively, and each is provided with a lock. The two doors of the sacristy are of the same redwood material, each having one leaf, and provided with locks. The church is whitewashed inside and outside. The walls inside are painted with a border above and below. The entire chancel and a great part of the ceiling are also painted. The whole floor is a pavement of adobe flags.

At the end of the month, Serra returned to Monterey. He arrived at his mission headquarters at Carmel in early June, and he sent Father Diego Noboa to Santa Clara to replace the deceased Father Murguía.

Serra continued his work in Carmel, but recognizing that he was dying, sent for Palóu who arrived at Carmel Mission on August 18. Serra arranged for the carpenter at the presidio to prepare a coffin for him. He asked to be anointed while seated on a little stool made of rushes.

On the morning of the feast of St. Augustine, August 28, he was visited by Captain Don Joseph Canizares, who had been a friend since the first expedition of 1769, and Royal Chaplain Don Cristobal Diaz, who had first met Serra at Monterey in 1779. Serra stood and gave them a warm embrace. After reminiscing he said: "Well gentlemen, I thank you that after such a long time, during which we have not seen each other and after making such a long voyage, you have come from so far off to this port to throw a little earth on me."

Serra prayed and accepted a cup of broth. He took it and, after giving thanks, said, "Now let us go to rest." He walked to his little room, took off only his mantle, and laid down over the blanket covered boards which served as his bed with his holy crucifix at hand. All except Palóu, thinking that Serra was going to sleep and rest since he had slept very little the night before, went out to eat. Palóu, a little uneasy after a short time, approached Serra's bed to see if he was sleeping:

> *I found him just as we had left him a little before, but now asleep in the Lord, without having given any sign or trace of agony, his body showing no other sign of death than the cessation of breathing; on the contrary, he seemed to be sleeping. We piously believe that he went to sleep in the Lord a little before two in the afternoon, on the Feast St. Augustin (August 28) in the Year 1784, and that he went to receive in heaven the reward of his apostolic labors.*

Serra was 70 years old when he died at his beloved Mission San Carlos. He had lived a religious life for 53 years, thirty five of which he spent as a missionary. So ended the earthly life of one of the first participants in the Santa Clara saga.

Chapter Two

COMMERCE

Malarín, Fatjo, Wade and Wilson

The subjects of this chapter witnessed monumental change in Santa Clara. Mariano Malarín saw the mission town from gold-rush days until just before the turn of the century. John Fatjo's small grocery served the community from the 1870s until it was transformed into a Safeway store in the middle of the 20th century. The Wade and the Wilson businesses began in the shadow of World War I, survived a massive urban renewal upheaval in the 1960s, to continue to the present time.

Santa Clara was not solely dependent on its small businesses however, and there were a number of large employers. The Eberhard Tanning Company, which had been in existence under another name since the mission period, produced and shipped hundreds of thousands of pounds of animal hides every year up until the 1930s when the demand for leather goods declined. The Pacific Manufacturing Company produced milled lumber work, par-

The Malarín Family

Juan Malarín arrived in California in 1820 as master of the ship *Senoviano*. In 1824 at Monterey he married Josefa Estrada, the daughter of José Mariano Estrada and Ysabel Arguello. The Malarín family became grantees of large ranches in the Salinas Valley and held many official positions in Monterey, the capital of Alta California.

The Malaríns sent their son, Mariano, to study at Fort Vancouver and later he attended college in Lima, Peru, where he studied languages, mathematics and jurisprudence. Upon the death of his father, being the eldest son in the family, he was obligated to leave Lima at 22 years of age in 1849 and return to Monterey, California. He served in various civic positions, including that of judge and supervisor, and was elected a member of the California State Assembly in 1859 and re-elected in 1860. His written memoirs are at the Bancroft Library at the University of California, Berkeley.

Mariano married Isidora Pacheco in 1859. She was the only surviving child and heiress of Francisco Perez Pacheco who owned enormous landholdings containing over 150,000 acres, including *Rancho San Luis Gonzaga* and the area of the Pacheco Pass. After their marriage, Mariano and Isidora lived in Casa Pacheco in Monterey, now one of that city's historical landmarks. But California's former capital did not

Refugio Malarín Spence Fatjo, daughter of Mariano and Isidora (Pacheco) Malarín. Courtesy the Fatjo family to the Austen Warburton Collection.

offer the opportunities it had in prior years, so in the mid-1860s the Malaríns moved to Santa Clara. They built their new house at the southeast corner of Washington and Santa Clara streets, near the homes of their relatives the Fatjos and Arguellos.

Malarín supervised the family's extensive land holdings and also became a distinguished member of the San José bar. He was a business associate of Edward McLaughlin and John E. Auzerais in the San José Safe Deposit Bank. Malarín was named president when the bank was organized, and he held that position until his death in 1895. In 1917 the bank was sold to the Bank of Italy, which later became the Bank of America.

Malarín was also a co-founder of the Madera Flume and Trading Company and for a time served as its president. Malarín's colleagues in business were people of considerable local importance including McLaughlin, who came from Pennsylvania to Nevada City, California, and

Mariano Malarín (1827-1895), married Isadora Pacheco in 1859. Mariano's sister, Refugio, married Antonio V. Fatjo. Malarín was President of the San José Safe Deposit Bank. Courtesy the Fatjo family to the Austen Warburton Collection.

Isadora Pacheco heiress of Francisco Pacheco who owned Rancho San Luis Gonzaga and the area of today's Pacheco Pass (Highway 152). Courtesy the Fatjo family to the Austen Warburton Collection.

in 1868 moved to San José, where he became a leader in its financial development until his death in 1919. Another Malarín business colleague was Caius Tacitus Ryland, a San José attorney who had come to California from Missouri in 1849 and later married a daughter of Peter Burnett, the State of California's first governor. Ryland's brother-in-law was William T. Wallace, chief justice of the Supreme Court of California.

Malarín's wife died in 1892 and was the last of the Pachecos to be buried in the family crypt in the San Carlos Cathedral in Monterey. Mariano Malarín died in 1895, and is buried in the Catholic cemetery in Santa Clara. In 1896, a year after Malarín's death, the stockholders of the Madera corporation met in San José and chose new directors. Among them were David M. Burnett, Governor Burnett's grandson, and Charles F.

Wilcox, who had arrived in California in 1857, moved to Santa Clara and graduated from Santa Clara University in 1871 and became a well-known attorney in the community. Another of the new directors was Dr. Luis Fatjo, Malarín's son-in-law and executor who also owned shares in the Madera company.

Malarín's daughter Paula married a physician, Dr. Luis Fatjo, in Barcelona in 1880. It is believed that Dr. Fatjo was introduced to the Malaríns by Santa Clara's Antonio Fatjo, who was married to Malarín's sister. His other daughter, Mariana, married Dr. Ramon Roca who was also a graduate of the medical school of Barcelona. The Roca family lived in a San José home on The Alameda across from the present YMCA. They had five children, including Monserrat Roca, who later lived in Santa Clara with her brother Ramon Roca. Both owned substantial property on Franklin Street. Another daughter, Lolita, married Dr. Rose of San José.

Although the family sold a number of the ranches, *Rancho San Luis Gonzaga* remained in the family until 1962 when the federal government took over some of the area for construction of the San Luis Dam and Reservoir. President John F. Kennedy took part in the ground breaking ceremony and members of the Santa Clara City Council, including Austen Warburton, a cousin of the Fatjos and Malaríns also attended. Paula Fatjo, the granddaughter of Dr. Luis Fatjo, continued in ownership of her share of the rancho, raising cattle and horses in the old family tradition with the Pacheco Pass and highway serving as remembrances of the family name and history.

The Fatjo Families

The Fatjo families have a long and illustrious history, not only in Santa Clara but also in Spain, particularly in Barcelona as early as the 13th century. Today's Fatjos can trace their lineage directly to the founder of the House of Fatjo, Bartolome Fatjo, long before the voyages of Christopher Columbus.

The first of the Fatjo family to settle in Santa Clara was Antonio Fatjo, born in Barcelona in 1828. He was the fourth son of John and Madsona (Ravento) Fatjo. At age 14, Antonio's health deteriorated and his family hoped that it might improve by taking an extended tour. Antonio left Spain by ship under the care of Dr. Noguera and traveled to South America. In Santiago, Chile, where friends of the family were in business, one of the local merchants offered him employment in their wholesale dry goods business. Antonio quickly accepted since he would inherit nothing from his parents under the primogeniture laws of Spain. He remained in Santiago for six years and married Mariana Salcedo, a member of a prominent Chilean family. They had five children: Antonio V., Amelia, John, Clorinda and Luis M. The eldest two were born in Chile, John and Clorinda were born in Santa Clara and Luis was born during a trip to Spain in 1861.

In 1849, Antonio decided to come north when he heard about the gold discoveries in California. He established a wholesaling and general merchandise business in San Francisco, and later, he became one of the first merchants in Santa Clara when he opened a store there. He built a large, rambling, one-story mansion at the northwest corner of Fremont and Washington streets. He was also a business associate of José Arques, a locally prominent cattle dealer.

Mariana, Antonio's wife, died in 1865 in Barcelona. In 1877, he returned to Santiago to marry Elisa, widow of Antolin Raventos (eleven years later, in 1888, Antonio's son John Fatjo would marry Antolin's daughter by his prior marriage, Teresa). When Antonio died in Santa Clara at the age of 73 just after the turn of the century, he was mourned by all as one of the community's "first citizens" and local businesses were closed for his funeral which was celebrated by Santa Clara University Jesuit Fathers Raggio and Kenna.

(Right) Teresa Farry Fatjo as a bride, 1902. Courtesy the Fatjo family to the Austen Warburton Collection.

(Far right) Fatjo hunting trip, circa 1890. (L to R) Antonio Fatjo, Dr. Luis Fatjo, John Fatjo, Joaquin Fatjo, Carlos Olvera, J.G. O'Brien, C. Acronico (child seated), and Antone Fatjo, Jr. (far right). Courtesy the Fatjo family to the Austen Warburton Collection.

(Below) Doubles tennis champions of Santa Clara County, circa 1890. Henry Luke Warburton (left) and Robert A. Fatjo (right). Courtesy the Fatjo family to the Austen Warburton Collection.

Tuco Fatjo standing in front with unidentified friends posing on an orchard ladder. Courtesy the Fatjo family to the Austen Warburton Collection.

ANTONIO V. FATJO AND HIS DESCENDANTS

The eldest child, Antonio V. Fatjo (1849-1917) grew up in Santa Clara and went into the family dry-goods business. He was instrumental in the reorganization of the Santa Clara Valley Bank and later organized the Mission Bank with his son, Robert A. Fatjo. He became the Santa Clara town treasurer, contributing his entire salary to worthy local organizations. Antonio V. and his brother John had disagreed with their father's decision to sell the old grocery store on Franklin Street to John Swinford and they bought it back. Thereafter, the store was known as "John Fatjo and Son," primarily run by John, until 50 years later when it was purchased by the Skaggs grocery chain.

Antonio V. married a widow, Refugio Malarín Spence, whose great grandfather was José Dario Arguello, one of the last of the Spanish governors of California. Her first husband had been David Spence, a member of a wealthy, prominent Monterey County family, with whom she had six children. Antonio V. and Refugio built a home at the southwest corner of Washington and Santa Clara streets. To their north, on the site now occupied by St. Clare's School, was the three story home of their cousin, José Ramon Arguello and his wife Ysabel, of the Alviso family, owners of a substantial grant of land at the south end of San Francisco Bay. On the east side of Washington Street was the prominent home of Mariano Malarín.

Antonio V. and Refugio had three children: Robert A., Eugene and Delfina. Delfina Fatjo, who never married, lived most of her adult life in her residence at 646 Washington Street in Santa Clara. Heartbroken on the sudden death of her mother, Delfina invited her Aunt Clorinda, an English teacher in Panama, to come and live with her. Clorinda did so and the two lovely ladies sat on the front porch entertaining friends and relatives as they lived out their lives in the Mission community. Delfina was particularly interested in her garden and generously assisted in a number of charitable enterpris-

Saint Joseph's School commonly referred to as "the brick school," located where Saint Clare's Church stands today. Several Fatjos were students there including Robert A. and Eugene. Courtesy the Fatjo family to the Austen Warburton Collection.

es. She also reared a beautiful child, Juliana Donovan, who lived at the residence for many years. Delfina died in 1968.

Eugene Fatjo became a banker and married Katherine Miner. The couple had one child, also named Katherine, who graduated from Dominican College in San Rafael and did graduate work at Stanford University. The younger Katherine married Gerald Harrington, a graduate of Santa Clara University who worked in San Francisco for the Coast Envelope Company. This couple also maintained a home in Santa Clara at 860 Washington Street. Their two children were Katherine and Candice, known to her friends as "Candy," and both attended school at Santa Catalina in Monterey and graduated from Stanford University.

Robert A. Fatjo was educated at Santa Clara University. He entered the real estate business in the office of Fatjo and Lovell at a time when his father was in the banking business. Later, in 1910, he was involved in the organization of the Mission Bank. He served as its president until 1917 when it was sold to the Bank of Italy, which had been started in San Francisco by A. P. Giannini. After the acquisition by the Bank of Italy, Robert Fatjo became manager of its Santa Clara branch, located at the southeast corner of Franklin and Main streets. The imposing two-story building was of Spanish style architecture, with the banking facility downstairs and upstairs offices rented to tenants. Over the years the upstairs area was occupied by a number of well-known professionals, including several dentists and attorneys. It was in these quarters that the noted law office of Dias & Kelly had its beginning. Joseph Kelly later was chosen as a Santa Clara Municipal Court judge and ultimately was appointed to the Superior Court bench.

Robert A. Fatjo was also vice president of the Santa Clara Building and Loan Association. His father, Antonio, had served as its treasurer. Robert was the first president and a long-time director of the Santa Clara Chamber of Commerce. Upon the death of his father, Antonio in 1917, Robert succeeded him as city treasurer for Santa Clara.

In the tradition of his generous parents, he gave his monthly salary to the city library, the Woman's Club, the Chamber of Commerce, and the firemen of Santa Clara. At that time, the fire department was basically a volunteer organization, with members of the community belonging to various hose companies. They were summoned from their regular jobs by horn blasts at the

City Waterworks to rush out and quell fires.

Robert A. Fatjo had a lifelong interest in athletics. He and his close friend, Henry Luke Warburton Sr., became noted tennis players in California and for a time were Santa Clara County doubles champions. Both men entered the banking business together; however when the bank was acquired by the Bank of Italy, Robert stayed with the Bank of Italy as its manager and Warburton took over the management of the community's other bank, the Mercantile Trust Company, a predecessor of Wells Fargo Bank.

In 1902, Robert A. Fatjo married Teresa Farry, the daughter of Patrick and Mary Farry. Patrick was born

Antonio Fatjo home at the southwest corner of Washington and Santa Clara Streets. Courtesy the Fatjo family to the Austen Warburton Collection.

Robert J. Fatjo, Bellarmine Coach, circa 1970s. Courtesy the Fatjo family to the Austen Warburton Collection.

in Ireland and during the great potato famine migrated to New York and later moved to California. The Farry home still stands at 824 Washington Street. Following their marriage, Robert A. and Teresa Farry Fatjo moved into a home at Washington and Liberty streets where both their children were born, Mary Teresa (1905), and Robert J. (1907). In 1911, the family moved into a new Spanish-style home at 616 Washington Street. Mary Teresa was educated in local schools and attended Notre Dame College in Belmont and later Sacred Heart College from which she graduated. She also did advanced study at Stanford University in the field of Spanish. Teresa Farry Fatjo, the mother of Mary Teresa and Bob, passed away in Santa Clara and is buried at the Catholic cemetery there. Some years after her death, Robert married Julia Golden, who was then employed as a teacher.

Mary Teresa Fatjo married Milton Premo. Around 1930, Milton A. Premo had come to Santa Clara County to intern at the county hospital under Dr. Doxie Wilson. He had attended Gonzaga University (where he was a schoolmate of Bing Crosby), and on completion of his academic work there, he attended Creighton University and received his medical degree. While interning at the county hospital, he was introduced to Mary Teresa. Following their courtship, the couple was married in 1933, at St. Clare's Church.

Robert J. Fatjo, the second child of Robert A. Fatjo and Teresa, was born in 1907 in Santa Clara. He attended grammar school at St. Joseph's School, commonly referred to as the "brick school," which was located where St. Clare's Church now stands. He then went on to study at the Santa Clara University prep school, which at that time was located on the Santa Clara University campus. In January of 1926, the school was relocated on the old College of Pacific campus in the College Park area of San José and was called Santa Clara University High. The school was renamed Bellarmine College Preparatory in 1928.

Upon Robert's graduation from high school in May 1926, where he was the first day scholar to ever hold the office of student body president, he entered Santa Clara University and graduated in 1930 with a degree in business administration. He spent the next seven years in San Francisco where he worked for the Bank of America, and continued his great interest in athletics, playing on the bank's tennis and baseball teams.

Robert, or Bob as he was known to his friends, began his coaching career in 1941 at Santa Clara University as coach of the freshman baseball team. He was blessed with a team of outstanding players and contributed to their development. Duane Pillette, later a resident of San José and member of the Board of Fellows of Santa Clara University, was his star pitcher and later signed with the New York Yankees. The student managers were brothers from Nevada, Paul and Bob Laxalt. Paul Laxalt became a U.S. Senator from Nevada. In 1943, Bob was named baseball coach at Bellarmine College Preparatory and continued to coach there for the next 27 years. In 1946, in addition to his coaching responsibilities, he assumed the duties of director of athletics and physical education instructor. Bob met Eleanor Salberg, a member of another prominent local family, and the couple was married in 1956.

During the summers, Bob was a member of the New York Yankees' scouting staff at tryout camps throughout the West. He also joined the staff of the *Examiner* baseball school, sponsored by the Hearst newspapers. In 1970, although he remained at Bellarmine as the director of athletics, he returned to Santa Clara as the freshman baseball coach. Outstanding players on this team included Bruce Buchte, who later played for the Oakland A's, and Tim Wilhelm, who later joined the San Diego Padres. Bob retired from Bellarmine in 1973 and was a member of the City of Santa Clara Parks and Recreation Commission for 12 years.

John Fatjo (1853-1936) another son of Antonio and Mariana Fatjo and the brother of Antonio V. Fatjo, was a kind, generous, giant of a man who lived in a lovely home located at the southeast corner of Catherine and Pierce streets in Santa Clara. The home still stands, although the lovely grounds that once extended for a block around it have been subdivided and developed. John was fascinated by birds and he constructed a large aviary which extended over several fruit trees. He and his wife cared for canaries, finches and many exotic birds. John also was an avid chess player and many of those who remember the family will recall seeing him sitting on the back porch deeply engrossed in chess matches with friends and relatives such as Dr. Roca. The children who visited the home while such matches were in progress were quickly encouraged to leave the players alone and to go else-where on the lovely estate to enjoy the birds, its beauty, the billiard table, the solarium, or even to explore the mammoth barn at the south end of the property in which for many years an old carriage and other equip-ment were stored.

John, along with his brother and son, and others in the family established a grocery store on the south side of Franklin Street between Main and Jackson streets. He was concerned with the welfare of families in the community, particularly turn-of-the-century immi-grants. He was ready to extend a helping hand, along with credit and advice, and there were many reports of the helpfulness of this kindly gentleman.

In 1888, John married Teresa Raventos (1864-1942) and the couple had two children, Teresa, who died in infancy, and Antonio, known as Tuco, who was born in 1890 in Santa Clara. Teresa was also well-known and beloved in Santa Clara. In contrast to her six-foot-six-inch tall husband, Teresa was short in stature and was frequently called Teresita. She was a gracious, kindly Spanish lady, an excellent cook and

John and Teresa Fatjo's home and yard on the corner of Pierce and Catherine streets in Santa Clara. Photographs by the author.

knowledgeable about the tasty foods of Spain. She fre-quently helped both friends and relatives arrange tradi-tional Spanish dinners. Her knowledge of Spanish histo-ry and beautiful fluency with the language was a source of help to many Santa Clarans who studied the lan-guage. She was often sought as a coach and a private Spanish teacher.

Prior to World War I, Amelia Coeke was employed to teach German at the local high school. With the out-break of the war, there was rising anti-German feeling in the community, in part manifested by the establish-ment of a "home guard" in which local men trained themselves with arms, marched in parades and prepared to repel any possible German attack. The school board

Ledger and scale used in John Fatjo's Santa Clara store. Photograph by Cliff Hunter.

Teresita.

Tuco married Jessie Malley, worked with his father in the store and, because the family had a large ranch on Skyline Boulevard in the Santa Cruz mountains, in the fall would harvest chestnuts, walnuts and apples for sale and for distribution to friends and family. In the winter of 1927, Tuco contracted pneumonia shortly after he became soaking wet gathering chestnuts. He died leaving two daughters, Antoinette (Toni) and Marcella. The girls were raised by their mother, who eventually moved in with her in-laws.

Daybooks from the old Fatjo store from the 1870s indicate that most of the families of Santa Clara at that time did their shopping with John Fatjo. Interesting entries in the journals show who purchased kerosene for the lamps and other supplies and food at what today would be considered bargain prices. On one occasion, a stranger went into John Fatjo's store and talked with John for a time. As the fellow went out he turned, seeing the giant Catalonian following him, and exclaimed, "I thought you were standing on a box!" John's store was eventually sold and became part of Skaggs chain, which later became Safeway.

Luis M. Fatjo and His Descendants

Luis M. Fatjo (1861-1924) a brother of Antonio V. and John, married Eliza A. Raventos (1865-1921), the sister of Teresa Raventos (John's wife). The children of this family included twins, Rosita and Conina, who died while young, and Emily, Anita and Luis George.

The story of the various branches and relatives of the Fatjo family indeed puts into perspective the rich Spanish heritage of Santa Clara as it developed and adapted through the decades to become the large and bustling city of today. The Fatjos have been involved in all aspects of its development and stand high in the ranks of those who have contributed generously and well to the Santa Clara saga.

felt compelled to terminate German classes in the high school and Miss Coeke was asked to teach Spanish. Unfortunately, her knowledge of the Spanish language was limited and in order to develop adequate skills to enable her to teach the class she sought out Teresita Fatjo. Miss Coeke was trained by Teresita to become one of the most effective language teachers in the Santa Clara school system. Miss Coeke, up to the time of her death, resided in her home at the southwest corner of Fremont and Jackson streets, a short distance from the Fatjo home. Miss Coeke never learned to drive, so she walked to school at the south end of town toward Bellomy Street and also walked to the Fatjo home some blocks to the west to take her Spanish lessons from

THE WADE FAMILY

The first member of the Wade family to settle in the Santa Clara area was Harry Wade, who decided that life on an Illinois farm held little future compared with the opportunities in California where gold had recently been discovered. With his wife Mary and their three sons, Harry, Richard and Charles, and their daughter, Almira, they set out from Illinois April 1, 1849, joining a wagon train traveling the northern route to Salt Lake City.

By the time the party arrived at Salt Lake it was too late in the season for wagon trains to cross the treacherous Sierra Nevada. Stories of the Donner party's tragic crossing three years before was still vivid in their minds. Supplies in Salt Lake were running low and the oxen and wagons were worn out from already crossing almost half the continent. In early October, however, a 100-wagon train with 400 people and about a thousand head of stock was assembled under Captain Jefferson Hunt. He decided to proceed southwest to Los Angeles, and from there the immigrants could head north to the gold fields.

Captain Hunt proceeded slowly to conserve supplies and the strength of the animals for the desert ahead. About 300 miles south, on November 4, with cold weather setting in and ice forming on the water buckets, some of the members of the party became impatient and opted for a short cut. The notion was encouraged by a mule pack outfit headed for the California gold fields via a short cut through Walker Pass. The packers carried a map which showed a good trail with water and grass. The short cut was untried, however, and unbeknownst to the party, Death Valley blocked the way. After much debate, when the time came to turn off for Walker Pass, only seven wagons remained with Captain Hunt.

One hundred wagons followed the new trail marked by fresh mule tracks straight west from present day Enterprise, Utah. What was at first easy travel came to an abrupt halt near the eastern boundary of

what is now Nevada, where the party encountered a steep cliff, descending several hundred feet. The mule tracks led straight down, but the wagons stranded on the ridge could not follow. Scouting parties brought additional unhappy reports and more than half the wagons turned back to the main trail to follow Captain Hunt.

The Bennett, Arcane, Wade, and Earhart families, occupying family wagons, employed a number of teamsters, including John Rogers, a frontiersman from Tennessee, and Lewis Manly, who accompanied the Bennett family. Manly later wrote of the experiences in a book entitled *Death Valley in '49*. Their party proceeded westward from Nevada, divided into several groups, each planning its separate assault on Death Valley. Some, such as the Reverend J. W. Brier family, struggled

Former Wade family home (Above) and warehouse (Opposite page) in Alviso. "H. C. Wade" is barely legible on the side of the warehouse. Photographs by the author.

route across the salt flats and the Panamint mountains to get to California. The Wades suspected that Rogers and Manly might not want to face danger again by coming back, so they decided to find their way alone. Slowly and carefully the Wades travelled from water hole to water hole, heading in a general southerly direction. By sending scouts to find grass and water and never moving forward until they saw signal fires that the next water was spotted, the Wade wagon moved slowly but surely toward Los Angeles. They found the Old Spanish Trail along the Mohave River near Barstow and crossed the Cajon Pass into Southern California on February 10, 1850. A historical marker along the Amargosa River claims the Wades went that way but there are other indications that perhaps Wingate Wash, to the southwest, may have been the route the family travelled.

The Wades obtained supplies at Los Angeles and headed for the gold country, where they panned for gold for a time on the San Joaquin River east of Madera. Deciding that farming might be better than gold mining, the Wades crossed the Livermore Pass to the Santa Clara Valley. Their first farm, purchased near Meridian Corners, was not successful primarily because of drought conditions. Harry then moved near Alviso where he bought a house and, together with his sons, went into the freight business. They built a wharf and a large warehouse to accommodate hay or other produce from throughout the valley to be transferred to boats and barges for shipment to San Francisco and other destinations. He also opened a hotel known as The American House. The freighting operation became a profitable enterprise because most freight for San Jose, Santa Clara, and the busy New Almaden mine area came and went by way of Alviso. Indeed, many predicted that Alviso would become a large city since several substantial homes were built and a watch factory was established. Later it was dubbed "New Chicago."

Almira Wade, Harry's only daughter, married

for almost two months before arriving in Los Angeles. Reverend Brier began the journey as a strong and vigorous man weighing 180 pounds. He weighed less than 80 pounds when he arrived in Los Angeles, suffering from an abdominal ailment. His wife, Juliet, almost singlehandedly brought her family through to Los Angeles. Members of other parties were not so fortunate, and many died trying to find trails through the valley of death. The Wade family and its wagon fared better.

The Wades followed a trail left by other parties, thereby conserving the strength of their oxen and people. On Christmas Eve the family camped a mile east of Furnace Creek. A few days later, while the Wades were camped near the Bennett-Arcane camp at Tooley Spring, Manly and Rogers were sent out to scout a

Captain John J. Ortley, who for a time was in business with his father-in-law shipping grain and hay out of Alviso. Another of the Wade's children, Harry George Wade, took over the dock and warehouse business and developed a stage route between Alviso and Monterey. He also provided horses for Wells Fargo stage coaches.

Winter flooding was common in Alviso, and family lore recalled that during the flood of 1851, Harry's son, Charles, spotted a large salmon swimming ahead of him as he was driving a team along the street covered with nearly two feet of flood water. He jumped from the wagon and clubbed the salmon with the butt end of his ox whip and proudly took the seven-pound fish home for supper. Charles E. Wade worked the family ranch and met Estefina Alviso, the daughter of Domingo Alviso and Maria Magdalena Pacheco. Estefina's widowed mother is said to have greatly disapproved of her daughter's marriage to Charles Wade, a fair-haired gringo and an infidel (non-Catholic). When Charles declined to become a Catholic, the wedding was called off and guests were left waiting at the family home in Alviso with no word of what had happened. The couple threatened to be married by a justice of the peace but permission was eventually obtained for a priest to perform the ceremony in the original Ygnacio Alviso adobe.

Estefina's grandfather, Juan Ygnacio Alviso, had been born in Sonora, Mexico, in 1772, the son of Spaniards Domingo Alviso and his wife, Angela Trejo. Ygnacio came with his mother, brother and sister as members of the Anza expedition in 1775-1776. He enlisted in the army and served in San Francisco. He married Maria Margarita Bernal at Mission Dolores in San Francisco on January 12, 1794. The family moved to Santa Clara, and later, in 1838, he became the grantee of *Rancho Rincon de los Esteros*. The family had 12 children.

Ygnacio had worked as majordomo at Mission Santa Clara. His accomplishments were recalled by diarist Navario Galindo:

Having built all the houses in the square for the use of the priests, he then built similar houses for the soldiers of the guard. As soon as these houses were finished he moved the priests to the new mission, as well as the soldiers and the officer in charge of the guard. He then commenced on the houses for the nuns and the young single neophytes, after which he commenced the building of the church. . . . The church was finished [and] it was whitened with plaster which the Indians brought and painted.

Nasario Galindo's recollections, as translated by Cristina Alviso Chapman

Don Ygnacio also made ploughs for cultivating fields. Supposedly he equipped 100 pair of oxen to till 1,000 acres near the mission. There was a good harvest of wheat, barley and also of beans, corn, garbanzos, lentils and other kinds of grain so that the storehouses of the mission were full. The priests told Ygnacio that they never wanted him to leave because he was so valuable to the mission enterprise. The crops were used to feed the priests and Indians and large quantities were also sent to San Francisco to sustain the soldiers at the presidio.

Reportedly, on one occasion, a great swarm of locusts threatened to destroy the crops. The locusts ate the green wheat, even the stems. Ygnacio, seeing that the prayers of the priests did not seem to turn the locusts away, mobilized several hundred Indian men and women. About 50 of them were told to bring dry hay and spread it outside the planted area. They brought blankets and, holding them by the corners, formed a large curving line while others armed with branches beat the ground to keep the locusts moving. The advancing line of blankets formed a barrier so that the insects were driven into the dried hay which was then set on fire to destroy the pests. So many locusts were killed that the Indians gathered them in bushels to dry them. "In this manner," recalled Nasario Galindo, "the crops were saved and a good harvest resulted."

Clara and Walter Wade, wedding photograph, September 30, 1934, from the invitation to their 50th wedding anniversary. Courtesy Austen Warburton Collection.

and county leaders donned cherry-red hats and boarded trains bound for cities all around the bay. At each stop, they passed out literature, pennants, flags and a plethora of promotional placards advertising the Cherry Festival at Santa Clara along with Santa Clara University's Mission Play which would coincide with the festival. Even some prominent in San José went along to promote the event like that city's mayor, civic auditorium manager Jay McCabe, and retail merchant Alex Hart.

Opening day of the 1913 festival exceeded all expectations when between 20,000 and 30,000 people attended and the *Santa Clara News* noted that the town looked like "a glittering fairyland of light and color." The festival was centered at the old town plaza park, where today's Mission Branch Library stands. But there were parades down the town's unpaved streets, aeroplane flights and concerts in the plaza park gazebo. The streets were lined with fruit exhibits and dotted with barrels of cherries, free for the taking. At night there were street dances and fireworks displays. A beauty contest was held, and the winner was crowned the Cherry Festival Queen.

Evidently the event was enormously successful, earning as much as $2,000 after expenses. Even though the 1914 carnival was equally well-attended, Santa Clara's Cherry Festival was never held again.

Although Ygnacio Alviso owned *Rancho Rincon de los Esteros* where Alviso is now located, he continued to reside at his house at Santa Clara Mission until he died in 1848, leaving a large estate. His will was witnessed by several prominent residents of the valley, including Alexander Forbes.

Charles and Estefina Alviso Wade had a large family which included Andrew, Daniel, William, Stephen, Charles (Chet), John, Walter, Mary, Charlotte, Elizabeth and Benjamin. William Welch Wade was born in 1872 on the 300-acre ranch operated by his father Charles on the San José-Alviso Road near Trimble Road. At the time, approximately 90 acres were devoted to strawberries, reportedly the largest strawberry farm in the world. In addition, many acres were planted in apples and pears. The children grew up working on the ranch. William, with his brothers and sisters, had inherited a share of the Wade ranch when Charles and Estefina died.

William married Mary Margaret Taylor who had been born in County Wexford, Ireland, in 1871. They had three children: Walter, Esther (who married Joseph Lamagna and settled in San Francisco), and John, who died in infancy. Walter Wade was born in San José on February 21, 1905. He attended St. Joseph's Grammar School and became interested in chemistry while in high school. At age 16, Walter approached the proprietor of Stephenson and Watson Pharmacy, then located at Second and Santa Clara streets in San José, asking for work as a delivery boy. The owner was impressed with the eagerness of the young applicant and hired Walter in 1921.

While working for Stephenson and Watson, Walter met Ben Fernish, who owned and operated the Ben Fernish Drugstore in Santa Clara. Fernish offered him a job at about the same time as another firm in Sunnyvale. After weighing both opportunities, Walter chose to go to work for the Fernish Drugstore in 1927. Ben's son was Dr. Charles Fernish, a local physician, and Walter was fond of both men.

In 1930, a huge explosion rocked the downtown neighborhood while Walter was working in the drugstore. There had been a complaint that there was an odor of gas in the nearby Mead Jewelry Store but no one was able to find the cause. The odor of gas persisted so Mead went to City Hall to report the problem. While he was at City Hall, a heater salesman called at his store. Mead's employee, Mr. Forsey, told the salesman that Mead was at City Hall and they were concerned about the gas problem. The salesman offered to find the cause of the problem and as he went into the back room, he lit a match. The resulting explosion killed Forsey, although the salesman escaped with only minor injuries.

Although one store stood between Mead's and Fernish's, the explosion felt like an earthquake in the drugstore. Mrs. Bowen, a clerk in the Fernish store, was so distraught by the blast that Walter had to revive her with smelling salts. When he went outside to see what had happened, he found the owner of a nearby delicatessen out in the street with a knife trying to find the man responsible for the explosion. The salesman escaped the knife-wielding deli owner, but suffered cuts because he had been blown through the store window in the blast.

In 1932, Clara C. Gorman stopped in the Fernish Drugstore to make some purchases. She met Walter and they agreed to attend a dance at the Old Hacienda Dance Hall in Almaden on Saturday night. Romance blossomed and the two were married in 1934, at St. Clare's Church. Clara's parents had been born in Ireland. They met in San José, however, and were married at St. Patrick's Church. They had seven girls and one boy born: Mary, Margaret, Ellen, Sarah, Teresa, Anne, Clara and Thomas.

Clara had attended Braly School and later Fremont School when the family moved into a two-story frame house on a 10-acre parcel of land on Clay Street near the present intersection of Clay and Jefferson. She attended Santa Clara High School in the old brick building on Washington Street. She was fond of a number of her teachers, including Catherine Graham, Bertha Wiltz, Muriel Steinhart and Charles Townsend. On graduating in 1924, she worked as a switchboard operator and as a clerk in the billing department for Pacific Telephone Company at its offices on the south side of Franklin Street across from the Jewel Bakery. Clara's father had worked for the City of Santa Clara as a teamster. For a time he drove wagons hauling gravel and during the summer months he drove the city-owned, horse-drawn water wagon with sprinklers to settle the dust in the unpaved streets. Both of her parents died before her marriage to Walter Wade.

In 1938, Dr. Charles Fernish, Ben's son, told Walter that the family wanted to sell the drugstore which his father had operated. Walter was given the first opportunity to buy the business because he had been a faithful and capable pharmacist and employee. Walter accepted the proposal and Wade's Mission Pharmacy was established. The store was located in an area that was to be taken over by an expansion program of the Bank of America, so in 1944 Walter had to find a new location. He moved into the Odd Fellows building at 1000 Franklin Street, on the southwest corner of Washington and Franklin streets. Wade's Mission Pharmacy continued to operate successfully in that location until an urban renewal program took over the heart of old Santa Clara in 1966 when it moved to its present location on the Franklin Mall. After years of serving the community, Walter decided that it was time to take life easier and in 1970 sold the pharmacy to Frank Pinheiro. Walter continued to work with Frank to help in the transition of the business and the continuation of the high quality personalized service which for decades had been the hallmark of his business.

Walter and Clara had one child, Gerald Taylor Wade, born in 1937. Gerald attended St. Clare's School and Bellarmine College Preparatory where he graduated in 1955. While at Bellarmine, Gerald was impressed by his Jesuit teachers and decided to enter the Jesuit order. In 1968 he was ordained a priest at St. Ignatius Church in San Francisco. He was assigned to teach at Loyola High School in Los Angeles and became the assistant principal as well. His fields of teaching were classic languages, including Latin and Greek. He received his advanced degree in philosophy at Gonzaga University in Spokane, Washington, and then taught at Jesuit High School in Sacramento. He was named president of Bellarmine in 1979. In addition, Father Wade served as a member of the Board of Trustees of Santa Clara University.

For decades Walter and Clara Wade contributed to the life and well-being of Santa Clara. As proprietors of Wade's Mission Pharmacy, at all times of day and night, they provided for the medical needs of the people of the community. They were also active at Saint Clare's Catholic Church. The Wades have been an important part of the Santa Clara saga.

THE WILSON FAMILY

William A. Wilson, better known as Bill, was one of Santa Clara's outstanding merchants for over sixty years. He and his wife Ursula also devoted themselves to many community activities. Bill served as chairman of the school board for many years and was also chairman of the board of Santa Clara Savings and Loan. Ursula served as president of both the Red Cross Association and the Santa Clara Woman's Club.

William A. Wilson was born in San José in 1884, to William Wilson and Marie (Ley). The elder Wilson worked for many years in the fruit brokerage business. When young William was about nine years old, his father died and he and his two brothers, Ralph and David, were required to help support the family. Their mother also found what work she could. Young Bill found a job working after school and on weekends for

Urban Renewal

Federal legislation in the late 1940s and early 1950s created the Urban Redevelopment Agency, which funneled money into local communities so that they could condemn and clear blighted areas. Besides eliminating slums, urban renewal sought to increase land values and produce greater tax revenues. Local politicians in cities across the country could not resist the temptation of rebuilding their community with federal money. There was a high price to pay, however, as the oldest parts of cities were bulldozed.

In 1958, the city of Santa Clara's application for federal dollars for urban renewal was approved and years of contentious debate ensued. At stake was an area called the "University Urban Renewal Project," bounded by Lafayette and Jackson streets and Liberty and Benton streets. Another proposal enlarged the area to extend from Lincoln Street to the Southern Pacific tracks and from Bellomy on the south to El Camino on the north. The federal government rejected the second plan because it's calculations were based on 1950 census data, not the special census in 1955 which indicated Santa Clara's population had grown by 500%. Santa Clara's redevelopment agency was the city council.

Proponents envisioned a modern Santa Clara. They claimed that 41 of 77 buildings in the project area did not meet provisions of a fire code. A consulting firm predicted that the redeveloped area would become "a place of history, pageantry, art galleries, libraries and coffee houses. . ." It would be years before officials acknowledged that these lofty expectations were unrealistic for a town of 80,000 residents.

Opposition to the urban renewal plan was primarily from the downtown merchants group. They were represented by San José attorney John Burnett who had been active litigating against annexations by some Santa Clara Valley towns. The only dissenting city council member to Santa Clara's urban renewal plan was Austen Warburton.

One vocal opponent to the urban renewal plan was downtown merchant and son of the bakery family, William Wilson, Jr. He testified as to the integrity of many buildings. At one meeting, Wilson was forcibly removed by officers when he exceeded the three-minute speech limit set by the city council. It is ironic to note that even though Wilson objected to the redevelopment project, his family business is one that survived urban renewal and prospered. Some merchants who did not voice their objections lost their businesses altogether.

An alternative plan that called for renovating and rehabilitating buildings was proposed by some downtown merchants, but it was never seriously considered. In 1961, over 150 merchants filed a suit against the redevelopment agency which was dropped a year later when a compromise removed a two-story building height restriction on new development. The compromise also allowed a period of three months for business owners to decide whether to buy back into the renewal project.

In February 1965, the walls came tumbling down when 19 buildings were razed. The first was the old Franck building, once owned by the prominent local family of the same name, which housed Menzel's Hardware Store and an upstairs dance studio. The Bank of America building, which since 1955 had been the Pereira Men's Store, was second in line for the wreckers' ball. Santa Clara Home Furnishers at Franklin and Monroe got a brief reprieve, but ultimately came down too. One photo journalist said the scene was "reminiscent of the aftermath of a London blitz." Five old homes were leveled at the corner of Benton and Lafayette to accommodate the Crocker-Anglo Bank.

The first property owners to repurchase land in the redeveloped area were attorney Austen Warburton, whose family had owned three structures, and William Wilson of the Jewel Bakery. Warburton planned to lease his building to Wade's Mission Pharmacy, Blake's Stationery, and Sam & Roy's Barber Shop. The Wilsons re-opened their bakery also as part of the new Franklin Mall.

In the late 1960s, Santa Clara University's President of the Board of Regents and San Francisco hotel magnate Ben Swig proposed a university-owned shopping center and professional center, something along the lines of Stanford Shopping Center. He made it clear that the university would intend to make it a money-making operation to create an endowment for the school. Swig had architectural drawings produced and named a number of potential tenants, including the May Company retail chain, a major grocery store, various specialty shops and a cultural center. However, Swig's ideas did not materialize.

Of all the possible alternatives, whether renewal or rehabilitation or even just leaving things as they were, no one predicted that most of the University Urban Renewal Project would sit vacant for almost twenty years. Visions of the future were clouded by the dollar signs that city officials simply felt could not be passed up. Developers did not materialize to purchase the former downtown to build a new city core. Ironically, James Viso, who had been a city councilman and an early advocate for urban renewal, twenty years later acknowledged that an error had been made in razing the old downtown. In 1978 he ended up buying six acres from the city that had never sold, and even then, there were no competing bids on the property.

the Breitweiser Baking Company, a San José bakery, where he learned the baker's trade.

In 1917, Bill married a San José girl, Ursula Fisher, the daughter of Joseph and Lena (Eberle) Fisher. During World War I, Bill served as an instructor in the Army Cook and Baker's School at the Presidio in San Francisco. In October 1921, when his military service was complete, Bill purchased the Jewel Baking Company in Santa Clara, renaming it Wilson's Jewel Bakery. His business grew and prospered at its Franklin Street location. The downtown urban renewal project in the 1960s forced its relocation to its present address on the northeast corner of Homestead Road and Monroe Street.

Bill was active with the Santa Clara Chamber of Commerce and also served for a time on the advisory

Wilson's Jewel Bakery on Franklin Street before the downtown was razed under an urban renewal plan in the 1960s. Courtesy the Wilson family to the Austen Warburton Collection.

Right: William and Ursula Wilson. *Courtesy the Wilson family to the Austen Warburton Collection.*

Far Right: Ursula Wilson and William Wilson, Jr. turn the first shovel at the groundbreaking for the current bakery at Homestead Road and Monroe Street. *Courtesy the Wilson family to the Austen Warburton Collection.*

board of the Bank of America. He also became a Mason, was a member of Siotos, and the Woodmen of the World. During his term as chairman of the board of the Santa Clara Savings and Loan, it grew and moved from small quarters on Franklin Street to its home office on Monroe Street. When Bill retired as chairman he was succeeded by William Prentice, and later the institution was acquired by Gibraltar Savings and Loan.

Bill also was elected to the school board, serving as its chairman for many years. During this period, the population of Santa Clara grew and new schools were built. One, located on Benton Street, was named the William A. Wilson School in Bill's honor. Bill's wife Ursula was also interested in community affairs. She served for many years on the board of the Santa Clara Chapter of the Red Cross, and as its president for several terms. She also was active in the Santa Clara Woman's Club, serving as its president from 1949 to 1951. The Wilsons supported the Boy Scouts, especially Troop and Post 77 in which their son Bill Jr. was actively involved. The bakery provided innumerable cookies and cakes for scouting events.

Bill and Ursula had three children. The oldest, Patricia (b. 1922), married George Morton Reitter of Sacramento with whom she had two sons, George, an accountant and investment manager, and Thomas, an employee at the Lawrence Livermore Laboratory. The second child, Ursula Ardeen (b. 1926), married Jack Gillam. They had five children: Alix, Greg, Gretchen, Matt, and Penelope. Ursula now lives in Honolulu with her second husband, John Marx, a mathematician.

The Wilsons' third child was William A. Wilson, Jr., born in 1935. Bill Jr. attended Santa Clara High School and graduated from the University of California in 1959 in the field of organic chemistry. He earned his Master's Degree in guidance and counseling at Santa Clara University in 1974. While at Santa Clara High School, he met Rosalie Ann Gangi, daughter of Valentine and Lucille (D'Amico) Gangi, and they were married in 1956. Her father, Valentine, was born in New York and moved to San José at the age of 16. His parents, Anthony Gangi and Rosalie Aiello, were from Palermo, Sicily. Rosalie's mother, Lucille, also traced her ancestry to Italy: her father Anthony D'Amico came to California via New York as well.

Bill Wilson Jr., following in the tradition of family community service, became active with many local organizations. He served on the board of the Triton Museum of Art and he worked with the Boy Scouts, including Explorer Post 77. Bill was elected to the Santa Clara City Council and also served as mayor. His service with the city covered an eight year span, during which he purchased his father's interest in the bakery and continued to operate that enterprise successfully.

Bill's interest in youth and youth problems led him to obtain a degree in counseling, and through his efforts the Bill Wilson Center was established in Santa Clara to serve the youth of the area.

Rosalie served as president of both the Santa Clara Junior Women's Club and the Santa Clara Woman's Club (1972-1974). She was involved with the Santa Clara Philharmonic and the Little League. She became a staunch supporter of the Triton Museum of Art, serving on its board and for three terms as its president. During her tenure on the board, the new Triton Museum building was designed and constructed, attracting nationwide attention.

Bill Jr. and Rosalie had two sons, William A., known as Alex, (b. 1959), and Kenneth M., (b. 1961). Both graduated from Santa Clara High School and both have worked in Wilson's Bakery from the time they were small children, learning the business from their grandfather and father.

Ursula Wilson died in 1965. Bill Jr., after taking an extensive trip to South America, discovered he had cancer and passed away in 1977. His father, Bill Sr., died ten years later. The Wilson family has been greatly respected by the entire community. They continue to contribute to the economic, social, and cultural life of Santa Clara that was of such great concern and interest to their forebears.

William Wilson, Jr., who served on Santa Clara's city council from 1963 to 1971 and as mayor in 1965. Photograph by Airi Kulpa.

CHAPTER THREE

POLITICS

FRANCK, HICHBORN, LEVIN AND VISO/SOARES

When Santa Clara was incorporated in 1852, it was governed by an elected five member board of trustees. The president of the board acted as mayor, and just before the Depression, the official title was changed to mayor. Early in the 1950s, the board of trustees changed its name to city council and by 1970, the mayor was no longer named by council colleagues, but directly elected.

Each of the central characters of the stories in this chapter held political office except Franklin Hichborn who was a political journalist of substantial influence in the Progressive Era in California. Again, the author highlights community service by politicians as well as their political careers. Warburton himself held political office and served on civic boards and commissions. He was on the planning commission in Santa Clara from 1950 until 1958, appointed to the city council in 1958, and elected the following year. He served in that capacity until 1963.

THE FRANCK FAMILY

The multi-storied mansion that for many years was the home of the Franck family stood at the northeast corner of Washington and Benton streets but was razed to make way for the Wells Fargo Bank building. Frederick Christian Franck Sr. was born in Wäschbascherhof, Bavaria, December 23, 1828. He made significant contributions to the Santa Clara saga.

At age 15, Frederick left school to learn the harness and saddle-making trade at Kaiserslautern. Two years later he emigrated to the United States, working at his trade in New York City making saddles for the United States government to use in the Mexican War. In 1848, he left New York to find more saddlery work, first in Buffalo, then Cleveland, Cincinnati and Louisville. Traveling to New Orleans he turned to chopping wood and clearing land to make ends meet. Hearing of opportunities in the West, he started for California in December 1851, traveling by ship to the swampy, malaria-infested Isthmus of Panama which he traversed on foot to catch a ship on the Pacific side. He arrived in San Francisco in February 1852.

The excitement of the gold rush drew Franck to the Sierras where he spent almost two years mining on the Yuba and Feather rivers, at Shaws' Flat, Murphy's Camp and Columbia. In the latter part of 1853, Franck decided that his gold mining endeavors were not as fruitful as he had hoped. He returned to San Francisco and established the second shop in that city for the manufacture of harnesses and saddles. In 1855, he visited San José and then moved to Santa Clara where he permanently established his harness and saddlery business. He was eminently successful, invested wisely, acquiring substantial property holdings, on part of which he built the lovely Queen Anne style Victorian mansion mentioned above. Bevelled glass was imported from Europe, a sweeping staircase installed and the home became a center of activity for family and friends.

Franck married Caroline Durmeyer at Santa Clara in 1857. She had been born in Wolfskirchen, Germany. Although Franck and his wife had eight children, only two grew to maturity, Caroline and Frederick C. Franck, Jr. The senior Franck was a member of the board of town trustees of the city of Santa Clara for eight years and promoted projects for the community's development. He helped to organize the fire department, whose volunteers served the city for many years, and held the position of chief for six years during the 1870s. Franck was also one of the incorporators of the Bank of Santa Clara County, serving as one of its directors and chairman of its finance committee.

In 1871, he was elected to the State Legislature on the Republican ticket and was re-elected two years later

Caroline Durmeyer and Frederick Christian Franck on their wedding day in Santa Clara, September 23, 1857. Courtesy Bea Lichtenstein Collection.

for a second term. He also served as a state senator in 1894–95. Secretary of State F. J. Brandon published a record about the 31st session of the California Legislature in 1895 which shows Franck as Republican Senator representing the 30th District of the state, which encompassed most of Santa Clara County. He was named as chairman of the Claims Committee of the Senate and a member of several other standing committees, including the Committee of Agriculture, Horticulture, and Viticulture, the Committee on Counties and County Boundaries, a Committee on Public Buildings, and the Committee for Public and Swamp and Overflowed Lands. He was active in state Republican politics and was chosen a delegate to the National Republican Convention of 1888 as a representative of the Fifth California District.

As with many pioneers, he became an active member in the Independent Order of Odd Fellows. The Odd Fellows promoted fraternal relationships among its members in order to help families cope with the death

Home of Caroline and Frederick C. Franck on the northeast corner of Washington and Benton streets. It was razed to accommodate the Wells Fargo Bank building. Photograph by Alice Hare from "Progressive Santa Clara" a pamphlet published in 1904.

of a loved one, provide education, and visit the sick. Affiliated with the Santa Clara Lodge, Franck passed through all of its chairs, and during his administration as Noble Grand the Odd Fellows building in Santa Clara was erected on the southwest corner of Franklin and Washington streets. Through the years, it was made available to other groups, such as the Eastern Star, the Rebekahs, and the Woodmen of the World. It also provided the site for the March 25, 1904 beginning of the Santa Clara Woman's Club, originally known as the Civic Improvement Society. To provide income for the lodge, street level stores were rented. The building continued to serve the Odd Fellows until it was demol-

Volunteer Fire Department

As early as Santa Clara's incorporation in 1852, local men cooperated as volunteer fire fighters. Sometime in 1854, the Methodist minister's home burned, killing his little daughter, which sparked more efforts to organize a volunteer fire squad.

Frederick Christian Franck was one of the townspeople dismayed by the house fire at the minister's residence. He called a meeting and formed the Tiger Engine Company, and was elected its first chief. He served in that position for a short period of time, but his influence rallied many more to participate in fire-fighting. In 1855 Santa Clara issued its first ordinance authorizing the volunteer fire organization. Their fire-fighting techniques were rather primitive, not much more than a bucket brigade, but members attended meetings and made plans in case of emergency.

In 1856, while Franck was fire chief, a benefit was held to raise money to purchase fire-fighting equipment. Franck enlisted the support of the Jesuits who had established Santa Clara University a few years earlier. Students and faculty of the school provided music for a full house audience for the benefit held at the new college theatre. It must have been a highly successful fundraiser, because shortly afterward the volunteers purchased a hand pumper

Tanner Hose Company, circa 1883. Those pictured were identified by Robert Roll in 1946 who lived longer than any of the others. Back row, left to right: Henry Schneickert, Ed Miller (foreman), Joe Leipett, Dan Cronin, Christopher Emig, I.J. Koehle, Albert Metzler, Charles Geockeritz, Bill Humbert, Henry Muckler, Robert Roll, Jim Rafferty, Chris Franck, Sam Helfgott, Fritz Keile, Henry Brothers. Front row left to right: Jacob Huber (in front of hose cart); seated: Jacob Eberhard, J. Bogardes, Morits Heinecke. Courtesy the Austen Warburton Collection.

engine and a 500-foot leather hose for about $1,500. Eventually there were several different "companies" of volunteers, including the Hook and Ladder, Tanner Hose, Hose Brigade, Hope Hose and Mission Hose companies. Monthly dues were collected, meetings held, and the companies sponsored community picnics where they often challenged each other in sporting competition.

In the waning years of the volunteer department, Jimmy Bacigalupi, who was captain of the Tanner Hose Company, was also saloon-owner and town mayor from 1941 until 1949. He owned Dergans Corner, a popular watering hole catering to Santa Clara University students, alumni and town officials. Evidently when a fire would break out in town, the fire truck driver would swing by Dergans Corner to pick up additional volunteer fire fighters who had been relaxing at the bar. Bacigalupi was on the town's board of trustees for a total of 14 years.

In 1949, the volunteer fire department was replaced by a paid force. The first paid fire chief in Santa Clara was Leonard George and he remained in that position until 1975. There were some hard feelings when the volunteers were disbanded because the comraderie was sorely missed, however many recognized that a growing population demanded a paid force. By 1950, the city's original old hand-pumper was prominently displayed as an historical relic in the de Young Museum in San Francisco's Golden Gate Park.

Maude and Fred Franck. Courtesy Santa Clara Photo Archives.

ished as a result of a city urban renewal project almost a century after it was built.

Franck visited his native Bavaria in 1870, and he had an opportunity to call on boyhood friends. He also made a tour of Europe, visiting points of historical interest. On returning to the United States, he expressed a firm belief that no region of the world excelled California as a place of residence. Franck died in 1902, two years after his wife Caroline had passed away.

Their daughter, Caroline Franck, received an education at the College of the Pacific and in 1892 married W. A. Laine, a member of another pioneer family prominent in the Santa Clara Valley. Laine family buildings still stand in Alviso. The Laines had one child, Franck, who together with his wife Marian, constructed a home on the southeast corner of Benton and Washington streets. Franck and Marian Laine had two children, Ruth and Franck Willis; the latter was killed in military service during World War II.

After W. A. Laine died, Caroline married "Johnny" Johnston and remained active throughout the balance of her life in civic affairs and in the Santa Clara Woman's Club. She was a frequent visitor to city council meetings in the upstairs council hall on the northeast corner of Franklin and Washington streets. Once, when paving the sidewalks was being discussed by the council, her conservatism brought forward the observation that if God had wanted sidewalks paved he would have done it himself.

Frederick C. Franck, Jr., the second of the Franck children, was educated in the Santa Clara schools. He was involved in business with the Enterprise Manufacturing Company, becoming its secretary. In 1900, he married Maude D. Shuld, a Sycamore, Illinois native. The home of Fred Franck, Jr., and Maude was built in 1905 on the southeast corner of Fremont and Washington streets and they lived there for the balance of their lives. This lovely two story home has been well restored and stands as a significant reminder of the achievements of the Franck family. The couple had two children: Delila, who married Earle Binder, and Fred Franck III, who with his wife, Elaine, built the existing cottage on the old Franck property on the east side of Washington Street between Benton and Fremont streets.

THE HICHBORN FAMILY

A historical interest marker rests in front of the Hichborn house at 1091 Fremont Street, Santa Clara. Placed in 1970 by order of the city council and the historical and landmarks commission, it reads:

American Colonial style adapted to California built in 1868 by Cary Peebles. Purchased in 1882 by F. Greenleaf Houlton of Houlton, Maine, father of Mrs. Franklin Hichborn. Franklin Hichborn was a journalist and political writer of national fame who exposed graft and corruption in California. His writings are preserved mainly at the University of California at Los Angeles.

INDEPENDENT ORDER OF ODD FELLOWS

The Independent Order of Odd Fellows (IOOF), established as a secret society in 18th-century England, was named for a group of men who performed odd jobs. They sought death benefits, workmen's compensation and an outlet to perform community service and good works. Today it is a fraternal organization made up of numerous "lodges" in cities and towns in twenty countries.

The first Santa Clara Odd Fellows lodge, No. 52, was established in 1856, just four years after the town's incorporation. The founding members were James Morgan, Zimri Garwood, Hiram Hamilton, John West, James Barr, William Cameron and a Mr. Smith and Mr. Baker. A dozen years later, the Santa Clara group built their headquarters on Franklin Street on land owned by member Mr. M. Whittle. The two-story structure had two store fronts on the first floor that were rented out to various businesses over the years. The earliest enterprises included a candy store and a billiard hall. The upper floor featured a large meeting room and a few smaller gathering rooms that other fraternal organizations or service clubs often borrowed for their own functions.

Some Odd Fellows membership requirements were that each was required to be ". . . a free white male of the age of twenty-one years;

Many great political leaders in California came to this house to seek advice and inspiration from the man who was a leader in the progressive movement that changed the course of government in the State of California.

Franklin Hichborn was born in Eureka, California, in 1869 to Frances Hunt and John Edwin Hichborn, a descendant of Thomas Hichborn who landed in Boston, Massachusetts, about 1640. Thomas was the great-grandfather of Paul Revere, whose midnight ride still stirs the imagination of students, and Robert Hichborn, Franklin's great-great-grandfather. Robert was a member of the Massachusetts Militia, and fought at Bunker Hill during the Revolutionary War.

With the founding of the new republic, Robert and his family moved to Maine where they set up a ship-building plant at Stockton Springs. Two generations later, Franklin's father, John Edwin, married Frances Hunt and in 1852 the couple came by ship around the Horn, to San Francisco. Later John Edwin established a produce business in Eureka and was involved in the construction of the city's first wharf. He had made and lost four fortunes when he died; Franklin was five years of age.

Franklin Hichborn made friends with the Indians in Humboldt County learning their language, and when he was 16, he took a job as an interpreter on a trading schooner that made seasonal trips to Alaska. After his mother moved the family to San José, he briefly attended the College of the Pacific. At age 20, when his family moved to Santa Clara, he entered Santa Clara University, studying there for two years.

He became interested in the law and decided to become a lawyer. He was admitted to Stanford University the year it opened, 1892. While a student at Stanford, he and a friend started a weekly paper, the *Santa Clara Index*. The paper waged a successful campaign for a city owned water system, but it folded in the panic of 1893. In debt from this experience, Hichborn quit school.

Franklin Hichborn at age 70. Courtesy the Hichborn family to the Austen Warburton Collection.

Mabel Hichborn. Courtesy the Hichborn family to the Austen Warburton Collection.

While he still hoped to become a lawyer, an event in San José changed his plans. An old family friend was arrested as a vagrant. Hichborn investigated the case and found that some corrupt people connected with the judicial system were profiting from the arrest of penniless men. He exposed the system in a pamphlet, beginning his lifelong career in journalism.

In 1894, Hichborn started the semi-monthly *San Jose Letter*, which laid bare the Southern Pacific Railroad Company connection with the political machine then running Santa Clara County. Hichborn was subjected to repeated denunciations from opponents and the *Letter* was driven out of business in 1897. Undaunted, he turned his sights to state political issues, first as a reporter for the *San Francisco Examiner*. In 1900, he returned to San José to publish the *San Jose Spectator* and from 1902 to 1904, he edited the *San Jose Herald*. He was the news editor of the *Sacramento Union* from 1904 to 1906, and worked for a number of other papers during his career, including the *Sacramento Bee*, the *Stockton Record*, the *San Francisco Chronicle*, and the *Fresno Expositor*. From 1906 to 1927 Hichborn

Hichborn house, local point of historical interest, 1091 Fremont Street, Santa Clara. Courtesy the Hichborn family to the Austen Warburton Collection.

worked as both a writer and a lecturer on political and economic subjects, publishing the *Legislative Bulletin* in Sacramento from 1915 to 1917.

Hichborn became well-known for his regular column in the *Sacramento Bee* about the political activities and affairs of the state, and he received particular notice for *Stories of the California Legislature*, his series of volumes on the 1909, 1911, 1913 and 1915 state legislative sessions. *Harpers Weekly* especially praised Hichborn for these works:

> To Franklin Hichborn, more than to any other journalist, is due the sweeping tide of political reform in California. The stern facts, marshalled in his "Stories of the California Legislature" for three successive sessions, have been fatal to those condemned

*by them. In the preface to his latest book, The
System, he says "It is my purpose—as far as it lies in
my power—to keep the cover off." In that phrase
lies the temper of his service. Dispassionate as a
recording angel, keen as a detective hero, he does
not need to muckrake but is content to let the logic
of his facts bring their own unsparing conclusions.
While the traditional "machine" of his generation
was still dominant in California, he saw that it was
not so important to know what was done as to
know how it was done; so he merely turned the
clock around, took out the back and showed the
voter how the machine worked. In other words, for
the last six years he has devoted himself to telling,
without fear or malice, the record of every man in
the Legislature, on every important measure; to trac-
ing the influences of special privilege through lobby
and hall; to laying bare the hidden and interwoven
roots which produce corruption.*

It has been said that Hichborn's "voice and pen
have ever been at the service of justice, truth and right,
and he has conducted several statewide publicity cam-
paigns of great value in their salutary effort on public
morals." In a 1912 campaign, his writings contributed
to the defeat of an attempt via an initiative proposition
to restore racetrack gambling in California. His work in
1914 was instrumental in bringing about the ratifica-
tion of the "red light" abatement act and, in his
brochure published in 1920 on "red morals" he
opposed the social evil of communism in Europe and
America. He was a staunch advocate of national prohibition of alcoholic beverages plus an early advocate of
public control of the state's water resources and hydro-
electric power.

Hichborn's *The System Uncovered by the San
Francisco Graft Prosecution* exposed political corruption in San Francisco and contributed much to cleaning
up that city's political situation in a struggle which

*The Hichborns celebrate their 50th wedding anniversary,
1948. Courtesy the Hichborn family to the Austen
Warburton Collection.*

occured in the wake of the 1906 earthquake and fire.
Francis J. Heney, who conducted the San Francisco
graft prosecution, said of this work,

*I have read The System with deep interest. It is the
only accurate and complete account of the San
Francisco graft prosecutions which has ever been
published in any form. Mr. Hichborn has performed
a most important public service. The perpetuity of*

Dean B. McHenry, Chancellor of University of California at Santa Cruz (left) commends Hichborn's lifelong contributions at a California Pioneers of Santa Clara County dinner at the De Anza Hotel, San Jose, 1962. Courtesy the Hichborn family to the Austen Warburton Collection.

republican institutions depends upon the masses being able to secure correct information, and to thus acquire a correct understanding of the underlying causes of corruption and of bad government in our cities, states and nation. The System will make plain to every intelligent reader just what these underlying causes of corruption and bad government are. It should be read by every person in the State above the age of 12 years. It is a clear, logical, sane and fair history of one of the most important periods in the life of San Francisco.

While Hichborn received many similar commendations for his work, some from national periodicals like *Collier's Weekly*, he was not without his critics. On one occasion in San José, one of his articles offended some folks enough that they accosted him in the street and threw him into a horse trough!

Hichborn and his friends inspired the movement early in this century that swept California to break the old controls of California politics and to provide a greater and more direct power to the people. Leading these reforms were the direct democracy tools of the initiative, referendum, and recall, but a number of other important constitutional amendments and legislative enactments also were adopted. Reformers succeeded in enacting blue sky laws, regulating securities sales, controlling public utilities, providing workmen's compensation, establishing minimum wages for women and children, instituting civil service, and pushing forward conservation of natural resources. Partisan politics, which contributed in many areas to a type of "bossism," was deemed unwise on the local political level and elections within the counties were made non-partisan. Successful reform propelled Governor Hiram W. Johnson to national prominence, first in 1912 with an unsuccessful bid for the vice-presidency as Theodore Roosevelt's running mate under the Bull Moose Party, and then through his service from 1916 until his death in 1945 as a United States Senator.

Early in his career, Hichborn met Mabel Houlton, daughter of Greenleaf Houlton, and granddaughter of the founder of Houlton, Maine. They were married in Fresno in 1897, and acknowledging his historic ancestry, their eldest son was named Paul Revere Hichborn (1898–1961). Generations of students at Santa Clara High School knew Paul as an outstanding biology teacher who held his students to high standards. He was also involved in other activities, including raising gladiolus in the vacant lot across the street from the old Block Packing sheds on the El Camino near Scott Boulevard.

OLD BILL BROWN

Old Bill Brown had been a Hichborn family friend for years, since their days in Eureka. At that time, he had survived as an itinerant tinker, mending pots and pans and making repairs on small household items. In the Santa Clara Valley, he turned to seasonal farm labor as his source of income.

He was quite disgruntled one season when he was repeatedly arrested for vagrancy. Even as he was making his way out of the county, he was picked up again, and thrown into jail. While incarcerated, he learned, and later recounted to young Franklin Hichborn, that under California law, the local constable earned $2 for every arrest of a vagrant, and the local trial justice earned $3.

With some research in local records, Hichborn discovered that in 1893, the Santa Clara justice, who by the way was a well-respected neighbor of the Hichborn family, earned $1,641 for prosecuting "tramps." The constable had earned almost $2,000 for making arrests. The sums were astounding to young Hichborn.

He tried to have his findings published in his own *Index*, but his partner refused, fearing loss of all their advertisers, and Hichborn was bought out of that paper. Then he took his story to the *San Jose Mercury* where the publisher threw Hichborn out of his office demanding, "What in hell do you think the *Mercury* is anyhow? A reform sheet?"

Hichborn did have some local supporters in his chess club however, and they financed the printing of the story and sent it through the mail. Hichborn suffered second thoughts about publishing his exposé even though it was completely true, and spent a sleepless night worrying for the safety of the local justice. He did not want any violence to befall the constable or justice. The morning of the mail delivery, Hichborn packed a revolver in case he needed it to protect the subjects of his exposé. As he walked toward Main Street, he saw a crowd gathered outside the justice's office near Franklin Street. What he found was the local justice shouting and threatening to sue Hichborn for libel, surrounded by a crowd of well-wishers anxious to show their contempt to Hichborn. The young journalist was completely befuddled that the public was not appalled by the double-dipping officials.

Ultimately, the tide of public opinion turned and California law was changed, in no small part due to the efforts of Franklin Hichborn, so that justices of the peace and constables were no longer paid for each criminal arrest, but paid salaries.

Paul's wife was Edith Bean and he was survived by one child, Robert Hichborn.

Franklin and Mabel's second child, Deborah, born in 1900, was educated in local schools and married David T. Rayner, an orchardist who also became the agricultural commissioner for Santa Clara County. They had two children, Donald E. Rayner and Drusilla R. Jones.

A third Hichborn child, Drusilla Hichborn, was born in Sacramento, in 1904. She was also educated in local schools and in remembering her youth in Santa Clara said:

> I grew up in Santa Clara in the same big old house my mother grew up in. My father had offices in San Francisco and commuted by train. He was away a great deal, but was usually home on week ends. In Santa Clara of that day—dirt streets, hitching posts at the gates, big barns, huge yards, chickens, rabbits, dogs, cats, coons in cages, the huge houses of the Spanish families, and the deep sense of belonging made it a memorable childhood. There was even a secret stairway in our house. Like other old homes of the time, fig trees were trained to make rooms for outdoor entertaining in the summer.

Drusilla graduated from the last two-year Normal School in California and, after teaching two years in Pasadena, she returned to San José State College for her B.A. Degree. She taught in San José schools, worked as a curriculum consultant in the central office, received her M.A. Degree from Stanford, and then taught at San José State. She also taught at Fresno, San Francisco and Sonoma state universities, served as consultant for some 30 years to the Sonoma County school office, and became active in the National Council of Teachers of English. Even though Drusilla moved to Santa Rosa, she held a life membership in the Santa Clara Chapter of the Eastern Star.

Franklin and Mabel also had twins, Mabel and Frances, born January 31, 1907. Mabel died while young, but Frances was educated in local schools and studied librarianship at San José State College, later marrying George Purser, an engineer. They had two sons, Roald, a well-known Seattle glass artist, and Eric, an officer in the Merchant Marine. Frances was associated for many years with the library at Humboldt State College in Arcata, making her home nearby and later moving to a cottage at Trinidad, overlooking Trinidad Bay. When she retired as the reference librarian at Humbolt State, she continued to spend her time working with the area's Hoopa Indians. Frances passed away in 1981.

Franklin Hichborn insisted on accuracy in reporting, and his daughter Deborah remembered his concern for the protection of the memorabilia he accumulated over many years. She assisted him in preparing a massive autobiography and in preserving his pictures and records. His study, located at the front of his home, was lined with autographed pictures of such noted California political figures as Hiram Johnson, the governor and later U.S. Senator, and Herbert Jones, a state senator who pressed for legislation protecting the state's water resources and who was active in many Santa Clara County organizations.

Hichborn was a member of the San Francisco Press Club, the Commonwealth Club of San Francisco, Liberty Lodge 299 F&AM of Santa Clara, and the National Economic League. Besides his rigorous work writing, he particularly enjoyed his garden. Many of the trees and shrubs that surround his home at 1091 Fremont Street in Santa Clara were planted by him between 1905, when he moved in and his death in 1963. His neighbors often saw him working in his garden and sharing his flowers and plants. He also enjoyed his summer cottage overlooking the ocean near Capitola where he collected many marine fossils from the nearby beaches.

At a dinner given in Franklin's honor by the

California Pioneers of Santa Clara County in 1962, the year before he died, Dean B. McHenry, first chancellor of the University of California at Santa Cruz, praised Hichborn in a moving tribute as one of the great figures in the history of the state. Franklin passed away on December 28, 1963, and Mabel died in February 1971 in Santa Rosa. Many of his papers are filed in the Hichborn Room at the UCLA library, while others are kept in the library of the University of California at Santa Cruz. The Hichborn family's contributions to the well-being of their community and state remain a significant part of the Santa Clara saga.

THE LEVIN FAMILY

Edward Levin and Margaret Ross established their family in Colorado where he worked as a railroad conductor. They had four children, two of whom became important in the story of the city and county of Santa Clara. Al Levin was born in Leadville, in 1898, and his brother Ed was born two years later in the same town. The family moved west to San José in 1920 and Edward Sr. got a job as the chauffeur for the director of the California Jesuits, the Jesuit Provincial.

Al took after his father's earlier career and worked for Southern Pacific Railroad starting as a switchman and later becoming yard master. His employment with the railroad extended from 1920 to 1963. During that time he worked with the morning and noon Daylight trains that gained much fame traveling daily from San Francisco to Los Angeles and back along the coast route. The powerful orange colored train with great view windows, comfortable seats, and dining cars made only a few stops along the way, a stop at San José being one of them. Leaving San José at about 9:00 in the morning, one would arrive at the Los Angeles terminal at about 5:00 in the afternoon. The run became one of the most popular passenger runs in California.

When Al began to work for Southern Pacific, the San José depot was located on Bassett Street, between

Ed Levin (left) and Father Bernard Hubbard, "the glacier priest," in Alaska, 1950. Courtesy Hubbard Collection, Santa Clara University Archives.

Market and North First streets. To enable the trains to get back on the San Francisco-Los Angeles lines, it was necessary for the train to back out from the depot and relocate itself on the appropriate line. The turntable by Cinnabar Street facilitated the turn-around. The aging building needed replacement and the new San José depot was constructed on Cahill Street in 1936 and remains at that location today. It was part of Al's responsibility to assist in making the change between the two stations. The last passenger train arrived from San Francisco at 11:00 p.m. at the old station one night, and thereafter all arrivals were transferred to the new one on Cahill Street. Al met many people while working for the railroad, including Clyde Arbuckle who once worked at the old express office and who became a local writer and historian. He also met two San José station masters, Guy Hassen and O. Phelps.

Some time later, Al met Frances Chapman, a local girl whose parents were William and Laura Chapman, her father a carpenter by trade. Anticipating their marriage, Al looked for a suitable house. He purchased one at 896 Madison Street in Santa Clara and following their wedding in 1937, the young couple moved into their new home.

As time went by, Al became interested in the politi-

Ed Levin using a typewriter with an ice cake as a table, surrounding by village children. King Island, Alaska, 1938. Courtesy Hubbard Collection, Santa Clara University Archives.

Bernard Hubbard, S.J., after a particularly grueling expedition, circa 1920s. Courtesy Hubbard Collection, Santa Clara University Archives.

cal affairs of Santa Clara and in 1957 ran for a seat on the city council and was elected. He served until 1961 and in the last year of his term was chosen mayor by his fellow councilmen. At that time, under the charter of the city, the seven-person council was elected at large, with those receiving the highest votes elected to whichever seats were open. Then council members would select one of their number to serve as mayor.

During Al's tenure, the council acquired 25 acres of land off El Camino Real for a new City Hall and other public buildings. Previously, the City Hall was situated on the northeast corner of Washington and Franklin streets in a two-story building with a central stairway and lovely marble siding. The city council chambers were upstairs in the southeast corner of the building and the city clerk and related offices were in the northeast corner. The first floor of the City Hall contained courtrooms; one having been occupied by Judge Charles Thompson, a long time justice of the peace and city attorney. In due course Judge Thompson retired and was replaced as city attorney by Robley Morgan, whose office was also located on the first floor. To the rear of the courthouse, with a back entry way, was the Santa Clara jail with its dank, barred cells under the supervision of the police department, whose offices were also located in the building. The city library had been located on the west side of the second floor until it moved to its new quarters in 1955 in the plaza on Main Street. Mary Mulhall served as librarian in those days.

While Al was on the city council, he and other council members became concerned over possible encroachments by neighboring cities and acted to protect the limits of Santa Clara by pushing them to Stevens Creek Boulevard. It was also at that time that a

The town's first library was a small collection of books in Justice of the Peace Jones' office. A generation after incorporation in about 1870, the Santa Clara Library Association was founded and members paid dues to support a small library. The reading room and its 300 books were located in the Odd Fellows building which had been built about five years earlier. A second reading room, sponsored by a temperance group, opened in 1879. In 1895 a Shakespeare Club started a book club too.

During the 1890s, two young Santa Clarans, Franklin Hichborn and Shelby Dodson, organized a lecture series to raise money for a library collection. They convinced Stanford University and University of California professors to speak for an honorarium of $25. The lectures were delivered in the basement of the Methodist Episcopal Church and evidently the series was a success. The young men netted $60 with which they purchased books and periodicals. Their reading room, in the Grove building at the corner of Liberty and Main streets, remained in use until the building was devastated by the 1906 earthquake.

At the turn of the century, there was a growing feeling that a library needed to be truly public, and not sponsored by any particular religious or social group. However, Santa Clarans defeated a vote for a public library in 1902. It would be the first of several times that people in Santa Clara would refuse to support a library even when outside funds were available.

Philanthropist Andrew Carnegie offered grants to communities across the nation during this period to construct public libraries. Many of the "Carnegie" libraries remain today as historic buildings. Santa Clara was offered the opportunity for a Carnegie grant, and Judge Bond offered to donate a building site and 500 books. But the town board of trustees decided the town could not support a library of that size and the offers were not accepted.

The board approved a small library to be housed in the Franck building, which after the earthquake moved to the old town hall. It operated on a shoestring for years, and when the new town hall was built at Franklin and Washington streets in 1914, was relocated there. The room was furnished by heavy old tables and chairs rescued just before Mariano Malarín's former home was razed. In 1938, a $12,000 bond issue came before the voters to build a library. The federal Work Projects Administration would fund a great deal of the new building. Again the voters cast dissenting ballots. A bond issue was on the ballot twice in the early fifties; both failed. Santa Clarans simply would not support a public library.

In the 1950s, the city council made budgetary arrangements to have a public library built in the old plaza park off Lexington Street and the 7,900-square-foot building opened in 1955. Within a few years it was obvious that even this was too small for the growing population, and indeed Santa Clara had "the smallest per capita appropriation and spent the least per registered borrower than any city in the Bay Area." Finally in 1959 voters supported a library bond issue. In 1965, ground was broken at a Homestead Road site for a larger public library.

The Franck Building housed a small library on its second floor for a brief period early in the 20th century. Sometime after the 1906 earthquake, the library was relocated to the town hall. A Nelson photograph from "Progressive Santa Clara" a pamphlet published in 1904.

An expedition to Alaska, Ed Levin (far right) and Fr. Hubbard (second from left). Courtesy Hubbard Collection, Santa Clara University Archives.

served as Grand Arch Druidess.

Al's brother Ed attended Stanford University and San José State where he gained recognition as a football lineman. Ed became acquainted with Father Bernard Hubbard, the famous "glacier priest" of Santa Clara University through his father who worked for the Jesuit Provincial. Father Hubbard made many trips to Alaska exploring, photographing, mapping, and studying the region. He became nationally recognized as one of the foremost students of that territory. Hubbard invited Ed Levin along on several of his trips and Ed became one of the major participants in the Hubbard expeditions. Apparently Ed was the first person to descend into the smoldering crater of Mt. Anikahak shortly after its eruption in 1931. During World War II, Hubbard provided substantial information to the government in connection with military activities in Alaska.

Ed's last trip to Alaska with Father Hubbard was in 1952. While on one of the Hubbard trips, Ed met Ruby McNeil, a native Kentuckian living in Alaska. Ed and Ruby married in Juneau, Alaska, but established their residence on Holly Drive in San José.

Ed, like his brother Al, also became interested in the political scene and ran for a seat on the Santa Clara County Board of Supervisors. He was elected for four terms and served as chairman in 1960-1961. At one point, a joint meeting was held of the county board of supervisors, then chaired by Ed Levin, with the city council of Santa Clara, then presided over by Mayor Al Levin. It was indeed a memorable occasion for the Levin family!

Ed was particularly interested in augmenting the county park system. While inspecting a park near Mountain View in 1965, he suffered a heart attack and died. In 1969, the Ed Levin Park near Milpitas was dedicated in his memory. His widow Ruby shared memories with her brother-in-law Al and his wife Frances of the time when both of the brothers served their respective constituencies in the best interests of the people.

capable young engineer who had graduated from Santa Clara University, Donald Von Raesfeld, was chosen to serve as director of public works for the city of Santa Clara. Von Raesfeld later was hired as city manager and served in that capacity for 25 years until his retirement and election to the council.

Al Levin was a member of the Brotherhood of Railroad Trainmen, now known as the United Transportation Union. He and his wife Frances were members of St. Clare's Church where Frances served as secretary for the ladies auxiliary for about 40 years. She was also a member of the Druids and in 1965-1966

The Levins played an important part in the Santa Clara saga.

VISO AND SOARES FAMILIES

Joseph Soares, born in Portugal in the 1860s, was kidnapped at age six by his uncle and taken to sea on a whaling ship. The captain's Irish wife sympathized with Joseph and took care of him, teaching him what she could. He never saw his mother again.

Joseph grew up working as a whaler, but left his ship to work in a Boston slaughterhouse. He met Mary Souza, a young Portuguese woman from Faial, an island in the Azores. He was 23 years old and she was 15 when they married. They began a family which grew to 14 children, but after seven had died because of illnesses and the cold, damp climate of New England, they moved west to San Francisco, California. Among the seven children who survived to maturity, Nellie, the eldest, was born in 1889, Margaret in 1891, Mary in 1893, and Clara in 1895. Frank, nicknamed "Hoppy," was born in 1899, Jessie in 1903, and Evelyn in 1910.

Joseph had come into contact with a brother, Kelly, who lived in the Santa Clara Valley, and worked on the belts at the Lick paper mill owned by the Scott family. Kelly urged Joseph to join him, and the family moved down from San Francisco. Not too long afterwards, Kelly was killed when a belt in the mill snapped. Joseph's family was permitted to stay on at the mill for a short time, until just before the 1906 earthquake, when they moved to a house in Santa Clara on Alviso Street.

Eleven-year-old Clara Soares remembered that they lit their home with coal oil lamps. Just before the earthquake struck, she heard dogs barking, cows mooing restlessly, and chickens cackling. Her father exclaimed, "Earthquake!" He put all the children under the doorways and blew out all the lamps. The force of the quake knocked the entire contents of the house about, spilling dishes to the floor, and breaking vases which had been

Santa Clara City Clerk A. S. Belick (left) holds swearing-in ceremony for city council members in 1960. (Left to right) Austen Warburton, James Viso, Robert Simons and Maurice Dullea. Courtesy Austen Warburton Collection.

given to Joseph and Mary as wedding presents. Although Mary objected when Joseph blew out the coal-oil lamps, he explained that if the glowing lamps had fallen, the house would have caught fire. Despite the earthquake's severity, Joseph consoled his family. He did not believe it was as bad as some of the earthquakes back in the Azores.

In Santa Clara, Joseph got a job with the Southern Pacific Railroad, which had extensive lines and yards. A Mr. Connely supervised Joseph's work with the railroad, and because Joseph was a good worker, he was promoted to foreman. While out with his crew in 1917, however, he was struck and killed by the Lark passenger train. Mary was left to raise the children alone.

Nellie and Margaret both married and worked with their husbands in orchards owned by the Weston family. Nellie's husband, Antone Gorvia, worked for Sam Weston on the large Peraleda pear orchard near Agnew, and Margaret's husband, Manuel Pasqual, worked on the large Will Weston pear orchard on Kifer Road in

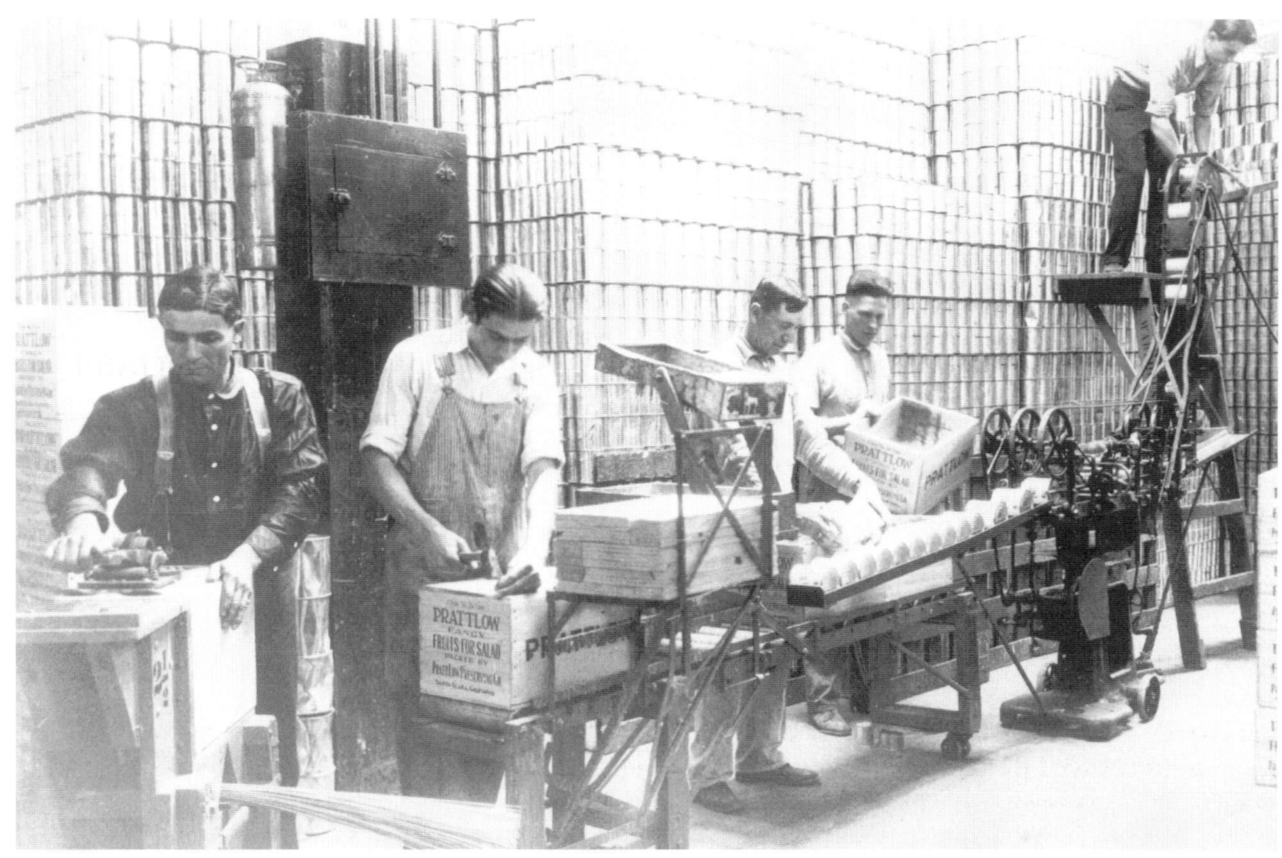

Pratt-Low box and can labeling room. Courtesy Bea Lichtenstein Collection.

Santa Clara. Nellie had no children, and Margaret had three: Clarence, Velma, and Joseph. Clarence also worked a while at the Weston ranch and later moved to Lancaster. Velma worked for a time in Lucca's Cafe, the popular Italian restaurant owned by the Gianninis on Grant Street near Franklin, then married and moved to San Diego. Joseph joined the National Guard, making it a career and settling in San Diego.

The third daughter, Mary, married Manuel Maderas in Santa Clara and bore one daughter, Dolores, who worked at the Bacon Ford agency in Santa Clara and then at Moffett Field. Dolores became engaged before World War II to Kenneth Stanford, who was in the service. He was stationed in the Philippines when the islands were captured by the Japanese, and he survived the Bataan death march as a prisoner of war. Upon his release and return after the war, he and Dolores were married and had three children: Kathy, Tad, and Patricia.

Joseph and Mary's next daughter, Clara, went to Midway School in Agnew with other children in her family. All classes from kindergarten through eighth grade were taught by Miss Keaton. Her punishment for children who did not know their lessons was to put

Santa Clara's water tower before the 1906 earthquake. Courtesy Bea Lichtenstein Collection.

soap in their mouths. A more pleasant memory was when Margaret Soares won 50 cents as a prize in a greasy pole climbing contest.

During the 1910s, the law did not require children to stay in school, and after the fifth grade, Clara quit to help her family by working. She took a job at Pratt-Low Cannery on Bellomy Street, where the beginning pay was 10 cents an hour. In 1917 Clara married Joseph Rose, but her young husband soon was drafted and killed in action in France during World War I. Years later Clara and other widows and members of the Gold Star Organization visited the Muese-Argonne Cemetery where Joseph and other war casualties were buried.

Clara continued to work at Pratt-Low. After some

years, workers at the cannery unionized, and the hourly rates were raised to 40 cents. Mr. Low and Mr. Pratt gave Clara an option to be paid by the hour or, if she preferred, to be paid for "piece work." Because she was fast and efficient, Clara elected to be paid for piece work and was able to make between $300 and $400 per week, a very large sum for that time. Rivalry among the workers was keen, and Clara remembers that a number of her fellow workers were jealous of her ability to earn so much. Workers on the canning lines wore gray uniforms and caps to prevent their hair from getting into the food, while foreladies wore blue uniforms.

Mr. Pratt, the owner, was a rather stout man who traditionally wore a brown suit and hat, was very nice according to Clara, and regularly greeted the employees with a cheery "good morning." Mr. Low, a tall man with graying hair, also had a friendly manner, as did another executive, a Mr. Wilder. Among the many people who worked during the height of the fruit season two foremen stuck out in Clara's mind: Bill Gavin and Mamie Debro. Others were Duncan O'Neal, who became a prominent San José attorney, and John Gourey, who became a priest. Pratt and Low eventually sold out to the Duffy Mott Co., which operated the cannery until Santa Clara University purchased the buildings on Bellomy Street to expand its campus. By that time Clara had worked in the cannery for 43 years.

Clara's youngest sister, Evelyn, also worked at Pratt-Low, but she left the cannery to marry Peter Turano in 1938. Ten years later, he opened Pete Turano Paint and Body shop on Stockton Avenue in San José, which he ran until 1970. Meanwhile, Evelyn opened Evvies' Beauty Salon on Franklin Street in Santa Clara, next to Dr. Robert Rogers' dental office. Peter passed away in 1979.

Clara's brother, Frank or "Hoppy," spent his younger years as wrestler, teaming up with "Babe" Pasquinelli, Babe's brother Henry, and Billie "Wise" Gonzales. Their wrestling team distinguished itself in competition, winning several trophies. After his wrestling years, Hoppy owned and operated the popular Flaxseeds Bar and Restaurant on Franklin Street. He developed an interest in politics and provided substantial support and advice for Santa Claran George Lyle when Lyle successfully campaigned to become sheriff of Santa Clara County. Later Frank entered politics himself, serving on the Santa Clara City Council with Pat Ryan and Peter Giannini.

Frank married Ann Malato of San José, and they had two children: Frank Jr., who worked for Amaral Plumbing Co. and later Amaral Mechanical Co.; and Antoinette, who married Steve Leahy, who worked for Standard Oil Co. Because of a deteriorating battle with cancer, Frank sold his saloon in the 1970s. He died in 1975.

Another sister, Jessie, also went to work early in life. As a young girl she worked as a clerk in O'Brien's Clothing Store on the northwest corner of Franklin and Main streets in Santa Clara. Among her friends were Margaret and Elizabeth Flannery, whose home was a block west on Franklin. Their uncle owned O'Brien's, which sold clothing and dry goods, Santa Clara's emporium of the time.

Jessie also had to shop for the family from time to time. She heard about a new butcher and decided to buy fish there. She met Charles S. Viso, a meeting which her family later described as "love at first sight." Charles and Jessie dated, and they became excellent dance partners, participating in contests and earning a reputation as champions.

Charles and Jessie married in 1926 and established their home on Tillman Street. Charles had been born in Cacamo, near Palermo, Sicily. He came with his family to Buffalo, New York, and when he was in his late teens, to Santa Clara County. He learned the butchering trade and worked in a shop on First Street in San José. Then he operated a market at Park Avenue and Race Street and later a meat department at the Genovese

Market at Grant Street and The Alameda. Eventually, Charles ran the University Market at Grant and Fremont streets, in a building rented from the S.E.S. Society, until he retired in 1968.

Charles and Jessie had one son, James J. Viso, who became one of Santa Clara's best known personalities. In fact, it was when James was an infant that his mother witnessed a bank robbery and shoot out in 1932. Bank robber Mark Monroe had robbed a bank in Santa Clara some years before, and it seems that he came back to rob another. After firing a shot inside the bank and scooping up handfuls of money from the startled and frightened tellers, he dashed out the door toward his getaway car. In the doorway he ran into Bert Yerkes, the owner of a feed and fuel business on Main Street, and Mrs. Viso. In the excitement, Monroe dropped some of the money as he darted across Washington Street toward City Hall. City Marshal Fallon happened to be walking in the opposite direction but he quickly got a gun from his parked car. Monroe hid behind automobiles parked alongside City Hall and an old western shoot out occurred. An army major who had served in the Spanish-American War heard the shooting, grabbed his gun, and dashed down Washington Street to join the fray. About the same time Judge Thompson, hearing the commotion from his office inside the City Hall, took his own revolver from his desk and was about to open fire from behind, when Monroe decided it would be prudent to surrender. He was arrested and eventually sentenced to state prison for his crime. The bullet marks in the old City Hall, however, remained until the wrecker's ball of urban renewal destroyed the grand old building.

The Visos taught their son the value of work when he was only five by encouraging him to sell newspapers. As a child James also worked on the Giannini farms in the Laurelwood area, irrigating, pulling weeds, and planting cauliflower and celery. On one occasion, when he wanted to go to the carnival which was periodically held on the S.E.S. Society grounds, he had to earn enough by parking cars in the family parking lot.

Charles and Jessie were people of great kindness and generosity. It was said that Jessie could never turn a hobo away from the door. She and Charles even took in and cared for one fellow, James Murphy, until he died, and when they could find no relatives, they buried him in their own family cemetery plot. The Viso house gained a reputation among "knights of the road" as a good spot to seek help. The family was even mentioned in a book written by one of the fellows they had helped.

Charles and Jessie frequently provided people with food and supplies from their University Market. When a friend pointed out to Jessie once that one of the recipients of this generosity took the food and sold it, using the proceeds to drink at a nearby bar, Jessie's response was typical of her: no matter what the mother did, the children still needed help. It should have been no surprise to James, when he cleaned out the University Market after his father retired, to find a drawer full of I.O.U.s which had never been collected. Charles Viso died in 1980 and Jessie passed away nine months later, ending another chapter in the Santa Clara saga.

LAW

THOMPSON, MOORE AND OWENS

THE THOMPSON FAMILY

The Thompson family is one of Santa Clara's oldest and most prominent, led by Isaac Newton Thompson, the first of three brothers to come to California. Isaac, accompanied by his lifelong friend, Zimri Garwood, crossed the plains by oxcart, arriving in Sacramento in September 1849 and in Santa Clara the next year. When he died a half-century later in 1913, *The Santa Clara Journal* called him one of "Santa Clara's noblest, honorable and upright citizens."

Isaac was the son of Squire and Charity Thompson who, for several years after their marriage in 1814, made their home in Preble County, Ohio. When the Treaty of Chicago opened southwestern Michigan for settlement, they headed for what is now Berrien County. En route a child was born in Union County, Indiana, on July 28, 1823, and named Isaac Newton Thompson. After a three month respite, they arrived in Michigan and the family purchased land which the government had shortly before acquired from Chief Pokagon. The Thompsons were the first American settlers in that part of the state and later they moved to Cass County, Michigan.

Isaac attended an academy in South Bend, Indiana, and on November 20, 1848 earned a "Certificate of Qualification" to teach. But by this time news of the discovery of gold in California was spreading across the country, and on March 14, 1849, Isaac and his friend, Zimri Garwood, (who also had been certificated as a teacher) started on their perilous trip across the continent. Some of the rivers they crossed had no bridges. Arriving at one of these streams, the men of the party were called upon to swim across. One tried, but the current carried him to his death. Then Isaac proposed that he and another man swim across the stream together. Both started, but only Isaac reached the opposite bank—the other weakening and turning back before he reached midstream. Their party eventually made it to Emigrant Gap on September 27, 1849, and shortly afterwards reached Sacramento.

After arriving in California, the two friends successfully worked a mining claim, but when the winter rains flooded their diggings, they went to Sacramento where they spent the next few months. Unfortunately, when they returned to their claim, it had been taken over by several claim jumpers. They did not challenge the persons working the mine, thinking it would be too dangerous. In any case, the winter in Sacramento had taught them that more money could be made providing services to the miners than in the back-breaking mining work. They opened a restaurant, grub-staked miners, and invested in the *Boston*, a steamboat plying the Sacramento and Yuba rivers. Later they sold their interest in the steamboat, each receiving $4,000 for his

Judge Charles Thompson. Courtesy Thompson family to the Austen Warburton Collection.

share. By the standards of that period, they were fairly wealthy men.

Apparently word of Isaac's financial successes reached other members of the Thompson family in Michigan. Isaac's mother had passed away late in 1849, and this left Squire, Isaac's father, with little to hold him in Michigan. He left his farm and home in the hands of his oldest son, William, and set off for California with two of his younger sons, Albert and Benjamin. After they arrived in 1850, Squire worked a mining claim near the town of Rough and Ready, and Albert and Benjamin were hired as teamsters. Squire suddenly succumbed to cholera, however, and was buried on November 22, 1850, with many others in a common grave in the Pioneer Cemetery in Sacramento.

That same year, Zimri Garwood visited Santa Clara. He returned to Sacramento with enthusiastic reports of the area and Isaac, Albert and Benjamin decided to dispose of their interests in Sacramento and follow Zimri back to the Santa Clara Valley. The four men lived together in a shack built on property somewhere between Santa Clara and Agnews, a temporary arrangement until better quarters could be found. Isaac was able to buy a part of the Tom Shore Ranch and later acquired the entire place. Isaac's father's estate needed attention so he returned to Michigan where he remained until 1856. He married Anna Smith in January of that year, and the couple planned to return to Santa Clara by way of Panama, thinking that the trip would be easier than the trek across the plains. Unfortunately, during the trip across Panama, a drunk fellow knocked over a fruit vendor's stand near a ticketing station. Some local people were infuriated and they attacked the travelers waiting to purchase tickets. The frightened passengers tried to barricade themselves in the station and Isaac was able to hold the door closed against the onslaught for an hour. He was shot in the thigh, however, and became weakened from loss of blood. When the mob rushed in, one of the waiting passengers was beheaded. They set their sights on Isaac and his wife when Isaac handed the ringleader his wife's gold watch and eighty dollars. The fellow called off his cohorts saying, "These are friends of mine. Leave them alone." The Thompsons survived the terrifying ordeal and continued on their journey to Santa Clara.

Isaac had a home built on Lincoln Street across from his friend, Dr. Henry H. Warburton, a man held in high esteem by the Thompson brothers. Isaac even

Owens, who heretofore had not been licensed to practice law in California. Owens passed the exam. The irony in the role reversal does not escape the author. Warburton taught at Santa Clara University Law School from 1946 to 1966.

(Opposite page) Native Sons of the Golden West installation team, February 16, 1921. Photo was taken in the meeting hall, second floor of the Bank of Italy building in Santa Clara, California. Standing: (left to right) Robley Morgan, George Koehle, Mark LaValle, Alphonse Ruth, Bill Schiller, Charles E. Newton. Seated: (left to right) Gene Sudenberg, Rudy Hipp, Andy Roll, Charles A. Thompson, and Al Nuttman. Courtesy Austen Warburton Collection.

Louise Rose (left) and Pauline Blanchard while students at San José Normal School, circa 1898. Courtesy Thompson family to the Austen Warburton Collection.

named one of his sons after Dr. Warburton: George Warburton Thompson. George served in the Spanish-American War, became a lawyer in Las Vegas, Nevada, as did his brother, Isaac Squire Thompson. The Thompsons also had four daughters: Martha (Keeler), Charity (Coffee), Anna (Huston) and Maybelle (Johnson). Isaac's wife Anna died, and in 1874 he married Emily A. C. Florey. They had one child, John Guy Thompson, who eventually lived in Goldfield, Nevada.

During the 1880s, Isaac Thompson was named Postmaster for Santa Clara and he and his brother Ben became partners in a local meat market. Ben had been born in 1831, in Pakagon, Cass County, Michigan. When he crossed the plains with his father and brother Albert, he was just eighteen. In California, he began farming and raising beef with his two brothers. For a time around 1870, the three brothers owned property in San Benito County and Benjamin and Albert lived in Hollister and Gilroy. However, they returned to Santa Clara to live out the balance of their lives.

In 1861 Ben married Emma Pennsylvania Kauffman, who was barely eleven years old, in an unusual ceremony where the bride and groom were mounted on horses. Emma was a direct descendant of Andreas Kauffman, a pioneer settler in Lancaster County, Pennsylvania, who took up land in Penn's colony in 1714. Ten children were born to Benjamin and Emma: Flora, Carrie, Ruth, Emma, Frankie, Benjamin, Charles, Robert, Una and Lester. The girls attended San José Normal School, where they were educated to become teachers and Charles and Robert enrolled at Santa Clara University. Charles entered the legal profession and later served as judge of the Justice Court in Santa Clara; Robert served many years with the county sheriff's office in San José. Lester attended the College of the Pacific when that institution was located in San José. Benjamin Jr. was employed as a clerk at the railroad station in Santa Clara.

Charles was a judge of the Justice Court in Santa Clara and an eloquent orator and was frequently called upon to make speeches supporting various charitable and civic events. A tall and imposing man, his office and courtroom were located in the old City Hall at the northeast corner of Franklin and Washington streets. Charles also played a role in the capture of the bank robber, Mark Monroe, in 1932 (Monroe's escapade is told fully in the Viso family story in Chapter Three).

Doctor Henry Hulme Warburton was an English-born physician who had served as a ship's surgeon before he settled in Santa Clara. He studied medicine at the London Hospital Medical Institute, then practiced under his father, also a medical doctor in England.

Dr. Warburton was Santa Clara's first doctor and was widely respected. He was a founding member of the local Odd Fellows Lodge, and a member of the Methodist Episcopal Church. In 1855 he married Catherine Pennell. They had seven children and one adopted child.

The Warburton home, built 1886, was at the corner of Main and Santa Clara streets. The first floor was used as pharmacy and medical offices, while the upper floor was living quarters. The house was moved to the San José Historical Museum and preserved as a medical office where thousands visit it every year.

Dr. Warburton was the physician for Santa Clara University students and he was enormously popular. When he died in 1903, flags on campus were flown at half mast.

The following is an excerpt from Zimri Garwood's journal which he kept while making the continental journey to California during the gold rush in 1849. For a time, he was in the company of the Thompson family. The second installment is from his journal which he kept while he lived in Santa Clara in 1851.

1849
MAY
TUESDAY, 22ND.
Clear and warm. We traveled on up the Platt and saw a small band of Pawnee Indians and passed the Pawnee village in the afternoon and found it disserted. It consists of a number of houses built in circular form, the frame or rib work of forks, ples and fine brush, woven to gether and coated with grass on the outside, the walls perpendicular eight feet high the rough running to a point at the center and the whole covered with earth. The whole exhibited a pyramidal form.

AUGUST
FRIDAY, 17TH.
Cloudy and like for rain. This morning was some excitement about a man being missing from an Ohio train. The supposition was that the Indians had got him. After traveling a few miles we met a company of twelve men armed to the teath going back in search of the lost man. To see men acting under the impression of these with that calm determination is better seen than imagined. We met the lost man going in great haste for he had heared of the excitement and expedition for his recovery. We met six Indianes who would have been victims of the exasperated whites if they had came in their way on the spot of the anticipated murder. We cross Martin's fork and took the bluffs for twenty miles. When we had reached the top of the first hill we had a hard storm of wind and dust and commenced raining as soon as the wind abated a little, and had quite a shower. We had rough road and half way through we came to some springs but the water sinks a short distance from the fountain. There was no opportunity for watering cattle and the trail was covered with dust and trash. The road lead through a canyon and was exceedingly rough and rocky. We decended the bluffs again after dark and camped on the bottom and trains continued to come in till some time in the night. We loosed our cattle and let them take care of themselves. I felt a little suspicious of the place on account of Indians from the opportunity which the situation country afforded them to do mischief, but they were dry and unmanageable and there was no alternative.

SEPTEMBER
SUNDAY, 16TH.
Cloudy and cool. We started early in the moring and continued our course south. Our road to day lay across open pine woods intercepted by small grass valley and some small streams of fine water. Late in the afternoon we struck Truckeys River again. WE followed up the stream some two or three miles and camped at the crossing, where the branch has become quite near a spur of a mountain rangeing towards the main ridge of the Sieranevada Mountain. This place is within a mile Truckeys lake being the head of Truckeys river. The spur of the mountain on the south is high and the north side steep and covered with a heavy groath of pine timber. Three quarters of a mile below this crossing we saw two cabins of the unfortunate Donathan party. [Donner Party]

Journal abruptly ends September 22, 1849
copied by Alda Garwood Jordan, 1950

1851, SANTA CLARA, CALIFORNIA

JANUARY
SATURDAY, 8TH
Clear & pleasant.
Ingaged all day at work about the house putting up beadsteads etc. The boys went to town & got some stove pipe.

SUNDAY, 9TH
Clear & pleasant. Went to Santa Clara to church. Went to Shearman's to church evening. Rush Mendenhall was up to see us.

MONDAY, 10TH
Clear & pleasant. Ingage at work about the house. Fixed up wrighting table, fixed stove pipe, reset stove, etc. Evening ingaged in making out papers for suits which were to come off in a sham court which we were about to institute.

TUESDAY, 11TH
Clear & pleasant. About home. The Farmer's Lyceum instituted a court & tryed me for not paying over the public money belonging to the Society. Sevral other cases were call but layed over. Court adjourn.

WENSDAY, 12TH
Windy blustery & cold. Set in the house all day a round the stove, on account of the cold. Tip Lindsey stay the day with us.

THURSDAY, 13TH
Clear & pleasant. Went to Mr. Thompsons got our shirts, paid Mrs. Thompson for washing.

Copied by Edgar C. Smith, 1983

In 1903, Charles was elected treasurer of Santa Clara and served in that office for two years. He was elected Justice of the Peace in the November 1906 election, defeating incumbent Judge Irving Herrington. Once elected as Justice of the Peace, Charles was re-elected again and again. When Clarence Coolidge resigned as city attorney of Santa Clara in 1930, Judge Thompson assumed that position also. In addition to these two positions, he carried on a private law practice. On April 1, 1950, Charles Thompson retired from the two governmental posts.

Judge Thompson, who lived at 1272 Market Street just west of the old Santa Clara High School, was active with many organizations and particularly with the Native Sons of the Golden West. As early as 1905, he was a delegate to the Grand Parlor. In 1927, he was state president of the Native Sons and participated in the laying of the cornerstone of the Los Angeles City Hall. Judge Thompson died on June 10, 1971, at the age of 91. In his obituary, he was referred to as one of the "most presidented" people in Santa Clara County because he had been president of at least a dozen local organizations during his lifetime. The Thompson family was a part of the Santa Clara saga through four generations.

THE MOORE FAMILY

Edwin Alphonsus Moore and his son Edwin Joseph Moore each served Santa Clara and its citizens for decades. The father was the superintendent of the Catholic cemetery, now known as the Santa Clara Mission Cemetery. His son was a quiet, hardworking city attorney.

The Moores can trace their ancestry back many generations to Yorkshire and Lancashire counties in England. Family legend holds that the family name was Shuttleworth, carried by a lad who was displaced during a period of religious strife centuries ago. Because he was a Catholic, according to the legend, the boy was adopted by a loving Irish Catholic family named Moore who gave him their family name and sheltered him through years of turmoil.

A descendant, Joseph Austin Moore, was born in 1854, in Sheffield, Yorkshire. Joseph, trained as a tinsmith, married Mary Alice Wilcock who was born in Buxton, Lancashire, England, in 1866. Some members of the Wilcock family moved to British Columbia, Canada, settling near Kamloops. Most changed the spelling of their name to "Wilcox."

After their marriage, Joseph Austin Moore and Mary Alice moved to Canada and settled in Ladner, British Columbia, where they owned and operated the Delta Tin and Copper Works. Joseph also operated a general merchandise store. All but two of their nine children were born in Canada, including Edwin Alphonsus Moore, who was born in 1899. His two youngest siblings, Herbert Thomas and Dorothy Marie Cecelia, were both born in Oakland, California, after the family moved to that city. While in Oakland and Alameda, Joseph operated grocery stores. During the 1920s, Edwin's mother, Mary Alice, encouraged him to work in the Santa Cruz mountains lumber industry, while he attended Heald's Business College in San José. The family established a residence at 941 Jackson Street at the corner of Lexington in Santa Clara. A devout Catholic, Mary Alice quickly became acquainted with Father Raggio, the parish priest at St. Clare's Church. However, Mary Alice died in 1926, and Edwin became the sole support of his invalid sister, Dorothy, and his aging father, Joseph.

Edwin had noticed a young woman, Eva Johanna Minton, as she passed the Moore home on her way to Santa Clara High School each day. Their friendship blossomed into romance, but Edwin was burdened by family responsibilities. He explained his plight to his sister Rose, who was then living in England and working in the rectory of their uncle, a Catholic priest. Rose agreed to come to Santa Clara to care for her father and sister Dorothy, taking title to the family home. Edwin and Eva were married in 1926 at the Santa Clara Mission.

Eva's father, Joseph Robert Minton, descended from a Portuguese family that settled in Brazil and moved to Santa Clara while Joseph was a child. When he was 24, he met Anne Berndt, the daughter of Hans Berndt of Denmark, and although Anne was only 16, they married. Joseph worked at the Santa Clara gas works which was later sold to Pacific Gas & Electic Company. He decided to go into business for himself and opened a bicycle shop at 957 Franklin Street, where he also sold Harley-Davidson motorcycles. His business was successful, he invested wisely in stocks and other securities and became quite wealthy. Joseph and Anne had two children, Naomi, who never married and died following a long illness in 1933, and Eva Johanna. Joseph died in Santa Clara in 1970 at the age of 89.

After their wedding, Edwin and Eva moved into a new home which Edwin had constructed on Jackson Street. Edwin had been employed by Pacific Manufacturing Company as a yard foreman for several years. In 1928, Father Raggio asked if he would become superintendent of the Santa Clara Catholic Cemetery. Edwin was assured that he would be in charge of the cemetery. He would earn several hundred dollars a month and would have an automobile for his personal use. In addition, he would be able to reside, rent free, in the mansion that Captain Lass had constructed on the cemetery property.

Edwin and his wife visited the Lass mansion and found that the huge house had been neglected for years. The building had great potential with its matching leaded windows, double front doors and grand living room. In the center of the living room was a large circular black iron chandelier suspended by ornate, matching black chains from the twelve foot ceiling. Wrap-around windows permitted ample light to flood the room. A large fireplace was adorned with pink colored ceramic

Edwin J. Moore, one-time Santa Clara City Attorney. Courtesy City of Santa Clara.

tile with sculpted Greek figures enhancing its beauty. The home was set back in a prune orchard over 100 feet from the easterly side of old University Street, now called Winchester Boulevard. There was a separately fenced garden area of approximately 3/4 of an acre and it was part of the responsibility of the Moores to see that the orchard was properly maintained.

The idea of living in a house at a cemetery caused Edwin and Eva some apprehension. Edwin decided to spend a few nights in the old mansion and he invited a

Austen
Miss Pogue

High Fifth
Feb. 15, 1928

My Ambition

When I grow up I want to be a lawyer. For I think it will be intersting work. And during my vacation, I will take the part of a travler and travel to differnt countries in which I will collect differnt things from differnt places. I will also take pictures of the places that I go to. Then I can put my collection together and have a museum. There I will spend my time after working hours.

Essay written by Austen Warburton in the fifth grade about his aspiration to become a lawyer when his teacher was Miss Jennie Pogue. Courtesy the Austen Warburton Collection.

Mr. Helm with his banjo and sleeping bag to join him. Both men survived the test and reported no evidence of ghosts. After the building was cleaned, the Moores moved in.

Edwin took charge of the cemetery office, although Manuel Roach, the former superintendent, continued to provide some assistance until his death. The prune orchard and berry farm located on the property were also managed by Edwin which produced income for St. Clare's Parish. The Lass house was slowly repaired and made livable.

The Moores developed friendships with a number of other Santa Clarans. One day a tall, curly haired young man drove a Standard Oil gasoline truck up the road to the mansion to make a delivery. The driver was Henry Luke Warburton and soon a long friendship began. Luke and his wife, Gertrude, and their son, Bob, went on vacations with Edwin, Eva, baby Edwin, and his little brother Joseph M. Moore.

Nye Farley and his wife, Georgie, also became close friends with the Moores. Nye worked at Pacific Manufacturing Company and Redwood Casket

Company on The Alameda. They lived on the northwest corner of Benton and Lafayette streets. Georgie was a member of the Eastern Star and was an accomplished pianist. Young Edwin, later the Santa Clara City Attorney, said that Mrs. Farley unsuccessfully attempted to teach him how to play the piano. However, Mrs. Farley was successful teaching piano to Rita, the youngest of the Moore children.

The Moores loved music. The children, who attended St. Clare's School, were taught piano by the nuns and also by Mrs. Farley. The family owned a piano and a foot-pump organ and the children particularly enjoyed pumping the organ and controlling the sounds with the mysterious knobs that could be pulled and pushed at will. In 1918, Olive Moore had married Dennis Layton, an orchardist and real estate agent as well as an accomplished banjo player, who regaled the family with his music. Young Edwin, however, thought that he should learn an instrument that could be played with more dignity and he was introduced to a B-flat soprano saxophone under the tutelage of Santa Clara University's master musician, Professor Clemens Van Perre. The professor visited the house with his black case which he slowly opened to reveal a shiny, silver saxophone on a purple velvet background. Edwin practiced with great enthusiasm on that wonderful instrument, and another life-long friendship with his music teacher was made.

During Prohibition, the town marshal, Peter Fallon, visited Edwin at the cemetery and reported a rumor that some illegal "booze" was stashed away in the old barn near the house. Pete said that he "certainly hoped that this was not true," and left. He never repeated the rumor or made another complaint. Old-timers remember what a great and understanding man Pete Fallon was and his inimitable style in law enforcement.

During the Depression, there was considerable unemployment and costs needed to be cut at the cemetery. Grave diggers found that there was a strata of gravel about five feet below the topsoil. Because individual cement vaults had become commonplace, money could be saved if the gravel for the concrete could be quarried right at the cemetery. Large gravel pits were dug and the bed of an old river that once traversed the area was uncovered.

As another way to economize, Ed cleaned the basement of the old mansion and converted it into an apartment to provide some family members, including his sister Olive, a place to live. Edwin's brother Herbert, who was beginning a wholesale produce operation in Santa Cruz, also lived there. Vegetable gardens were also planted which produced bountiful crops, rabbits were raised and the skins were sold. Squirrels were trapped and eaten with great gusto until the family discovered that this was not safe.

At the same time, the Moore children thought that they could earn money by raising violets which were sold to the Woodward Florist on Franklin Street for 10 cents a bunch. One of Mrs. Woodward's customers was so entranced with the fragrance of the violets that she placed a large order. The night before the delivery, to the dismay of the children who went to harvest the blossoms, Edwin had scattered fertilizer over the violet bed. To keep the children from losing the account, Eva hosed the flowers off with water as best she could. Unfortunately the water had also washed away much of the fragrance. Then Eva drenched the bouquets with her own violet perfume. The children took the bunches of violets to the shop and the purchaser expressed enthusiastic approval of the violets. The children were paid and the account was saved.

The Moore children were Joseph Minton, Edwin Joseph, and Rita Ann. All three were educated at St. Clare's School. Joseph Minton eventually moved to Watsonville. He and his wife, had two children: Michael who went into the field of electronics and married Denise Fisher and lived in Santa Clara and Dave who moved to Louisiana.

Rita Ann met Richard Wood, a graduate of the college of law of Santa Clara University, and married the young attorney in 1954. The couple lived in San Luis Obispo where Richard practiced law for several years and then was appointed a Municipal Court Judge and later a Superior Court Judge. Following his retirement, the family moved to Guadalajara, Mexico.

Edwin Joseph Moore was born in 1927, and after graduating from St. Clare's Grammar School attended Bellarmine College Preparatory. Ed had also served during World War II in the Army. He was trained at Fort Lewis, Washington, as an engineer but was assigned to the quartermaster corps on the U.S.T.A. *Republic*, a converted hospital ship that had become a troop transport. He attended Santa Clara University and in 1955 he earned his law degree. After he passed the California State Bar examination, he affiliated with the law firm of Hernandez & Holme, with offices located in one of Santa Clara's historic buildings on the southeast corner of Main and Benton streets. Ed also was appointed to the board of library trustees of the city and had great respect for Frances Klune, the city librarian. In 1957 Ed decided to run for city council and was elected in April with the highest number of votes cast for any of the candidates. Serving with Ed on the council were Mayor Nicholson, Joseph Rebeiro, William Kiely, Anthony Toledo, Victor Salberg and Al Levin.

Ed's military background and law profession contributed to his decision to work as a civilian for the Air Force at McClellan Air Force Base near Sacramento. It was necessary for Ed to resign his post on the city council and move to Citrus Heights, near the Air Force base. Upon Ed's resignation from the council, Austen D. Warburton was appointed to take his place. Ed worked in Sacramento for the Air Force for about one year, then Robley Morgan, who at that time was the city attorney for Santa Clara, needed assistance because of the increasing volume of legal work of the city. Ed came back to Santa Clara as the assistant city attorney, and

Post card of Pacific Manufacturing Company, Santa Clara, California. The wood products plant employed hundreds of Santa Clarans. Courtesy Post card collection, Stocklmeir Library/Archive, California History Center, De Anza College.

shortly thereafter, when Morgan died, was appointed city attorney, a position he held until his death.

Ed Moore met Josephine Estepa at a wedding in 1955. It was love at first sight. Following a whirlwind courtship, Ed and Josephine were married in 1956, in St. Clare's Church. Josephine's family had also resided in Santa Clara for many years. Her father, James Estepa, and her mother, Josephine Jurado, both had been born in southern Spain and came with their parents from Spain to Hawaii just like many other Spanish families. James and Josephine were married in Hawaii and three of their nine children, John, Joseph and Manuela, were born there. The other six children were born in Santa Clara after the family moved from Hawaii. All were educated in the Santa Clara schools.

James Estepa, the father of the children, worked on the Bracher Ranch near Pierce Street and also worked for the Block Company in their pear orchards. The family home was located at 1286 Pierce Street and still stands today. The children were encouraged to earn money by picking prunes, and cutting apricots, peaches and pears. The family raised chickens and rabbits and James was especially proud of his quail. Josephine made clothes for the children and was noted for her beautiful crochet work. When James, the father, died in 1945, at the age of 62, all of the children worked to help the family and one another.

Edwin and Josephine had three children. Edwin James, Stephen Berndt, and Joseph Austin Moore. With the heritage and the tradition of so many diverse ancestors, it is easy to understand how and why the two Edwin Moores made great contributions to the Santa Clara saga.

EDWIN JOHN OWENS

Santa Clara University was established in 1851 by Jesuit priest John Nobili at the direction of Bishop Joseph Alemany of San Francisco. It became a major institution in California, and the university offered law courses for many years under the direction of William C. Gianera, S.J. In 1933, the administration decided to hire a full-time law school dean, and after a search, Edwin J. Owens, a graduate of Harvard Law School was chosen.

Born in Lynn, Massachusetts, in 1897, Owens received his undergraduate education at Holy Cross College, finishing after he served as an infantry lieutenant in World War I. In 1922 he completed law school and was admitted the same year to the Massachusetts Bar. Owens practiced law for seven years and in 1929 became a professor of law at Boston College. While he was there, Father Gianera contacted him about the dean's opening at Santa Clara, which Owens agreed to take for an annual salary of $4,000. He was delighted with both the position and the opportunity to serve the university.

One of his first tasks was to increase the number of law school graduates passing the state bar examina-tion. Santa Clara's students had been having problems passing the bar examination, a requisite for the practice of law. Owens' interest, ability, and determination soon turned the situation around. Part of his effort required recruiting a team of excellent teachers. Among them were Joseph P. Kelly, who later was appointed to the Superior Court bench in Santa Clara County; Robert E. Hayes, an outstanding professor in the field of torts; George Stepovich, who taught corporations law as well as other subjects; and Leon Warmke, who taught courses in property. As time went on, Owens also recruited local attorneys to teach part-time for the university, including George Strong and Austen Warburton.

Owens instituted a more selective student admission program and he actively recruited capable students. One of his first recruits, Al Ruffo, was an engineering instructor at Santa Clara and also coached football in 1933. The university reportedly could not provide Ruffo with a salary increase for his coaching, so Owens persuaded him to accept free tuition at the law school instead. Owens recalled of the five students enrolled in Santa Clara's law school in 1933: "I had to flunk four of them. Al Ruffo was the only survivor. When that class went up for the bar examinations, Al was my sole representative. It was either 100% or nothing. Fortunately, Al passed." Ruffo became a practicing lawyer in 1937, involved himself in many civic activities, and became an advisory partner in the law firm of Pillsbury, Madison & Sutro in San José.

Owens and the faculty implemented the Socratic method of teaching and developed a close rapport with the students. Owens had a brilliant legal mind and became an outstanding teacher in such fields as contracts, evidence, and equity. Moreover, he was always open to friendly visits and discussions with his students. Indeed, in the years before World War II, the annual baseball game between the senior law students and the rest of the school became famous because of Owens'

Santa Clara University law student William Clark in a moot court trial, circa 1950s. Courtesy Santa Clara University Archives.

spirited umpiring techniques. Through the efforts of Owens and his faculty, Santa Clara's law school was accredited by the American Bar Association in 1937 and joined the Association of American Law Schools in 1940.

During the early years of Owens' administration, classes were held in O'Connor Hall and the law library was located in Varsi Library, some distance away. As enrollments increased, the distance became a problem. It became clear that a law building was needed. Under the guidance of Owens and the university administration, Bergin Hall was built and named in honor of Santa Clara's first law graduate. It provided classrooms on the second floor and administrative and

In the spring of 1942, a young San José man, Wayne Kanemoto, was finishing his final year studying law at Santa Clara University. However, he and his family, along with almost 3,000 Japanese-Americans, were required to meet at San José State's gymnasium on May 24 and 25 to register for relocation to internment camps under Executive Order 9066. Kanemoto boarded an evacuation train that departed San José destined for the Santa Anita (racetrack) Relocation Center. While his classmates heard their names announced at graduation, his name was called to report to Gila River, Arizona.

Kanemoto convinced authorities to allow him to sit for the bar exam in Los Angeles before leaving for Arizona. Each of the three days of the exam, he was escorted by a federal guard. After he arrived at Gila River, he learned that he had passed the bar, but he was not permitted to go back to California to attend the swearing-in ceremony. Kanemoto was sworn into the California bar from an Arizona internment camp.

In 1943, Kanemoto joined the armed services and later he became an intelligence officer. His superiors were surprised that he did not speak Japanese so they sent him to language school. Wayne Kanemoto returned to the Santa Clara Valley to practice law after the war, and in 1961 was named Santa Clara

Judge Edwin J. Owens. Courtesy Eymann Collection, Santa Clara University Archives.

faculty offices on the first floor together with an expansive library and moot court room, venue of mock trials and appellate arguments. An annual Coolidge Competition was established in memory of alumnus Clarence Coolidge, which provided impetus for law students to demonstrate their research skills, briefing abilities, and capacity to argue clearly in a court room setting.

As more and more students passed the bar examination and became successful in their law practices, the reputation of the school began to spread. Gifted students went on to establish notable careers as attorneys, legislators, and judges, among them California Supreme Court Justice Edward Panelli, United States Senator Paul Laxalt (R-Nevada), and Assemblyman John Vasconcellos (D-San José). Enrollment increased dramatically, yet the personal and friendly relationship between teacher and student remained.

During World War II the law school was closed, and Owens was appointed by President Franklin D. Roosevelt to the Alien Enemy Hearing Board for Northern California. In 1942 Owens passed the state bar examination, which was administered by his former student, Austen Warburton. After the war, Owens reestablished the law school, reinstated the faculty, and revised the course of study which was complicated by a tremendous enrollment of veterans attending the school under the GI Bill.

In 1953 Owens resigned as dean to accept an appointment to the Superior Court Bench in Santa Clara County. He presided over the appellate division of the Superior Court for several years and, with changing procedures, developed the pre-trial system. Among the many important cases over which he presided, the Park Center Urban Renewal case stands out. The city of San José sought to condemn several blocks of old homes in the downtown area from Market Street west to the Guadalupe River. Property owners in the area challenged the redevelopment law, but Judge Owens ruled in favor of the city. As a result, the old homes were razed and Park Center Plaza was built, which included banks, office buildings, hotels, and other facilities along widened, landscaped streets.

Owens' interest extended into many areas beyond the law. He was a director on the boards of the National Council of Christians and Jews, Catholic Charities of Santa Clara County, and John XXIII Senior Center. He received the St. Thomas More award from the University of San Francisco, the City of San José Distinguished Citizen's Award and an honorary doctorate of letters conferred by Santa Clara University in 1952.

Mabel Owens, the judge's wife, was also popular with those associated with the law school. The Owens home became a mecca for students, faculty, and legal scholars. Judge Owens never learned to drive so Mabel served as his faithful chauffeur. After she contracted cancer and died in October 1981, the Judge established the Mabel T. Owens' Endowed Law Scholarship Fund in her memory.

Santa Clara University Law School faculty, circa 1958. Standing (left to right) Austen Warburton, Robert Meiners, Patricia Coffman, William Sauers, Harold Everton, George Strong. Seated (left to right) Robert Hayes, Warren McKenney, Edwin Owens, and George Dunne, S.J. Courtesy Santa Clara University Archives.

Owens retired from the Bench in 1966 and practiced "of counsel" for some time. A respected judge, teacher, and legal scholar, Owens died in 1988 at the age of 91. He was described as a "legal genius" who had a deep understanding of the law, yet great humanity. He was an important contributor to the Santa Clara saga.

CHAPTER FIVE

IMMIGRATION

TOLEDO, SANCHEZ/CALLEJON, SAPENA AND RUIZ/MENACHO

Several social and economic factors contributed to heavy emigration from Spain around the turn of the century. The mortality rate in general was much lower than it had been before, although the infant mortality rate remained high. Quite simply, there were more people. The land could not sustain the vast numbers trying to eke out an existence on a tiny farm that in some regions were described as "handkerchief plots." Thousands flocked to cities and towns that were hemmed in by ancient walls and barricades.

Coupled with the population growth was a serious economic collapse beginning in the 1890s. During the previous two decades, Spain had enjoyed a relatively buoyant economy, especially in comparision with the rest of Europe, because of natural resources like copper and iron ore mined in the Basque region. In addition, Spain was the world's leader in the production of wine, primarily because the root louse, phylloxera, had infected French vines during the

THE TOLEDO FAMILY

One of Santa Clara's most popular mayors was Anthony (Tony) Rodriguez Toledo, born in Safaraja, a hill town in the province of Granada, Spain, in 1901. His father, Antonio, served with the Spanish cavalry during the Spanish-American War from 1895 to 1898. After his stint in the military, Antonio married Margarita Rodriguez and was a farmer. Tony was the oldest in the family. One brother, Joseph, was also born in Spain. In 1907 the family migrated to Hawaii, travelling by ship around South America on a long, difficult voyage.

In Hawaii, Antonio was placed in charge of the Spanish workers employed with a sugar cane company. More children were born, including Manuel, Placido, John, Frank, Beatrice, and Mary. The parents felt education was very important and insisted that all of the children learn both English and Spanish. After repaying the costs of the voyage to Hawaii, Antonio moved the family to San Francisco in 1913, and they moved to Santa Clara in 1918, where he worked in agriculture. During World War I, he was employed at Joshua Hendy Iron Works in Sunnyvale. Antonio remained a vigorous man, able to walk several miles a day until shortly before he passed away at the age of 93. His wife, Margarita, died in 1936 and they were buried in the Santa Clara cemetery.

While the family lived in San Francisco, Tony sold newspapers and later drove a taxi. When he came to Santa Clara he worked for the Clement family, becoming foreman of their cherry pickers. Later he worked for the Brown families, who had pear orchards. While working for the Browns in Santa Clara, Tony met Catherine Callejon, who had been born in Estepona, Malaga, Spain, in 1906 (her family's story is told with the Sanchez family). Tony and Catherine married in 1926, at Santa Clara Mission with the Reverend Father Raggio officiating. They took up residence at 1738 Harrison Street, where they lived for 29 years. Their son Anthony was born in 1927, and their daughter Margie was born in 1937.

Tony became interested in the grocery business and worked for a short time in the grocery store owned by John Fatjo on Franklin Street. Then he worked at the Blue and White Grocery Store (later called the Red and White Grocery) owned by the Sallows family on Franklin Street near the old City Hall. Eventually Tony purchased the store and operated it until the 1960s when Santa Clara's urban renewal program bought out and razed all of the buildings in the old downtown area.

Tony was also interested in politics. He began his political career when he was appointed in May 1943 to what was then called the board of trustees. He was

The Toledo Store, 975 Franklin Street, Santa Clara, California. To the left is City Hall. Courtesy Santa Clara Photo Archives.

elected in his own right the following year and served until 1949, when he was elected to the board of freeholders which prepared the new charter for the city and set the basis for today's Santa Clara government. At that time, the city government was based on a charter which called for a mayor-council form of government, but it was changed to a council-city manager form. Tony was chosen as mayor and served in 1950 and

1951. He was elected again to the council under the new charter, serving from 1951 to 1958 and again as mayor in 1958 and 1959.

Tony worked in his store next to the City Hall. Often he was called to take off his apron and go over to City Hall to transact business for the city. Always gracious, he could be called on to serve his community at any time of the day or night. Throughout his life Tony

1880s.

By the 1890s however, Spain's economy was in deep decline as phylloxera invaded Spanish vineyards. The diseased vines caused great conflict between tenant farmers who could not produce a crop, and landlords still demanding their rents.

The combination of more people, poor farming and crowded cities caused thousands of Spaniards to respond to emigration recruiters who promised land and a better life abroad. Although the rise of emigration began in the 1870s, it did not peak until 1912. In that year, 134,000 Spaniards left their homeland in search of a better life. Most of the emigrants went to Argentina and Brazil, some went to North Africa or France, and some went to America and Hawaii. One emigrant ship alone, the *Heliopolis*, transported 4,000 peasants to Hawaii.

The emigrant trade was rife with human rights abuses, and some reform laws in Spain sought to change that—however, not before thousands suffered harrowing voyages, vicious disease, inadequate rations, broken promises and in many cases, death.

Austen Warburton counted among his personal friends many Spanish immigrants and their sons and daughters. The path of these families is remarkably similar. Indeed some even left Spain on the same vessel, never meeting until settling years later in Santa Clara. The author's respect for the difficult choices faced by these families is obvious.

Santa Clara City Hall, circa 1920s. Courtesy the Austen Warburton Collection.

CITY HALL

Santa Clara's first official town hall was built in 1891, partially at the request of Santa Clara County which needed a branch jail. As it turned out, the county paid for the first floor and the town paid for the second. The two-story brick building was erected on a town-owned lot at the corner of Benton and Main streets. The second floor featured some offices, including that of Judge James Glendenning. Evidently his walls were decorated with dozens of b-b guns, appropriated from irresponsible gun-users. The decor served as a deterrent for repeat offenders. The building was razed in 1948.

During 1913, a new city hall was built at Franklin and Washington streets at a cost of $26,000, at least $11,000 over budget. It provided some amenities the town had heretofore gone without, like a fire proof vault for town records. The new building became headquarters for the board of trustees, the fire department, the library and the chamber of commerce. City hall suffered many scars over the years, not the least of which were bullet holes from the shoot out in 1932 between the city marshal, Pete Fallon, and bank robber Mark Monroe. This city hall was used until the 1960s when it was razed during the urban renewal program.

A new city hall was dedicated in 1964. The modern mission style building at 75,000 square feet was a far cry from the earlier models, costing almost $1.5 million.

worked with various organizations, trying to stimulate interest in the welfare of the people of Santa Clara. He was highly regarded by the Spanish families that lived in what was sometimes called "Spanish Town" on the northwestern side of the old quad area of the city.

Among the accomplishments he pointed to with pride was the beginning of the free rubbish pickup for the people of Santa Clara, a service established when he was elected mayor in 1950. In January of 1950, while Tony was serving as mayor, the Santa Clara University Bronco football team came home from defeating Kentucky in the Orange Bowl at Miami to one of the biggest welcome home celebrations that the college team ever received. Mayor Tony, believing that nothing was too good for the winning team, invited then-Governor Earl Warren to attend, and the governor accepted.

Tony was also instrumental in the acquisition of the property where the present police station and City Hall are located on El Camino Real. Although Tony had been devoted to the old City Hall at the corner of Franklin and Washington streets, he recognized that the growing community needed a better facility and urged the purchase of the new site.

Tony was also a member of the hose brigade and

hook-and-ladder company. On one occasion, a group of citizens petitioned the city council to remove the fire horn at Benton and Gould streets. Although Tony sympathized with the people living directly under the horn, he was disturbed by the suggestion and stated, "You people should get used to the way we live in Santa Clara. There were 180 signatures on the petition. That's one percent of the population. The whole population depends on those horns."

During the 1951 campaign for mayor, Tony strongly opposed the sale of any city lands to San José which wanted to annex Santa Clara land to expand the airport. He felt the expansion of the airport would create a physical danger and was unfair to industries already settled nearby. He also favored building two new firehouse substations, one in the industrial tract and one in the west side residential area. He pledged better bus service to residential areas. His record of keeping campaign promises stood him in good stead and he was re-elected by a substantial margin. In the same election of 1951, the new charter was adopted, which limited each council member to a one-year term until the new charter took effect the following year. Frank J. Barcells and Peter A. Giannini were also elected to the city council in 1951.

Tony was sometimes known as "Tough Tony" because of his love for the underdog. As his daughter Margie Del Prete once said, "He was short, but he was out there fighting for the little guy. Anybody who had a problem could talk with him and he took it right to the council." In 1958, Tony represented Santa Clara at the *Fiesta del Pacifico* at San Diego. In 1960, he was was named an honorary member of the Association of Friends of Father Junípero Serra of Petra, Majorca, Spain, by the president of the association, Antonio Bauza-Roca, and by the mayor of Petra, Pedro Aguilo. He was a charter member of the Spanish-American Voters League, serving as president and secretary. He was appointed to the Santa Clara County Grand Jury in

1972 and served as chairman of the Audit and Finance Committee. He also served several terms as chairman of the city's Senior Citizens Advisory Commission. He was affiliated with St. Anthony's Society, Redmen's Lodge, the American Association of Retired Persons, and the Golden Age Club. In 1978 he was elected first secretary of the Santa Clara Druids.

When he died from a sudden heart attack in 1980, all of Santa Clara mourned his loss. The city flags were flown at half mast in his memory.

TONY'S BROTHERS AND SISTERS

Joseph Toledo worked in San Francisco as a conductor on the transit system and later moved to Santa Clara, where he worked as a trucker with Lucky Lager brewery. Joseph married Ann Borusso of San Francisco. They had two children: Joseph, who became an engineer, and Frances,who married Roy Lusk.

Manuel Toledo married Bernice Blanco and worked as a custodian at Buchser High School until his retirement. Their children included Betty, who married Don Miller, and Robert, who graduated from San José State University, where he played football. Robert later became a coach at the University of the Pacific and U.C. Riverside. Placido Toledo, who worked as a mechanic at Stanford University, married Mary Gonzales and had two children, Richard and Emily. Following Mary's death, he married Connie Paniagua.

John Toledo worked as a custodian in the Sunnyvale school system and married Josephine Fernandez. They had two children, Becky and Kenneth. Frank Toledo first married Rose Fernandez, with whom he had two children, Debbie and Wayne. Following Rose's death, Frank married Mildred Koneic. He became one of Santa Clara's first paid firemen, along with Leonard George, Jerry Ledesma, and John Andrade. On his retirement from the Santa Clara Fire Department, Frank moved to Paradise, California.

Beatrice married Anthony Texeira. Their son, Dan, was employed by IBM. Mary married Joseph Sanchez, who was employed by the Gangi Brothers. Their children included Marilyn, who married John Fernandez, and Shirley, who married David Chadwell. Mary was employed for a time by the Marvel Cleaners.

THE SAPENA FAMILY

The Sapena family is another Spanish family that immigrated to the New World in search of opportunity and eventually settled in Santa Clara. Through hard work, all of the children were educated and developed into community and business leaders.

Antonio Sapena was born in 1882. He was the third child and eldest son of Vicente Sapena and

Sapena family, circa 1930. Left to right: Anthony, Frank, Carmen, Antonio, Maria, Teresa and Joseph. Courtesy Sapena family to the Austen Warburton Collection.

Chief of Police, Frank Sapena, circa 1970s. Courtesy Sapena family to the Austen Warburton Collection.

Theresa Pastore Sapena. They lived in La Villa De Andara, Provincia Alicante, Spain, a small village of independent farmers who worked the land as far back as Roman times. The Sapenas had six children.

Early one morning as Vicente was going out to the fields, a gun he was carrying accidentally discharged when his cart hit a bump. The tragic accident left Theresa alone to raise her small children. Although the oldest son, Antonio, had the responsibility of working the land, good friends who lived in Madrid offered to take him to the city where he could be educated. Theresa agreed, but a short time later Antonio became disenchanted with this arrangement and ran away to Barcelona, where as a boy of 12, he obtained a job working on a merchant ship as a cabin boy.

The company for which Antonio worked had vessels which stopped at Italian, Spanish, Portuguese, Central American and U.S. ports including Savannah, New York, and Boston. Antonio learned to speak Italian and became proficient in several Spanish dialects including Catalan, Majorcan, and Valencian.

Antonio worked for the steamship company for many years and once, when the company sent him to Costa Rica, he was entrusted to transport cargo to the Pacific side of the country where it was to be picked up by another ship. He contracted a severe fever, however, and almost died. When he recovered, the doctor recommended that he go north if he wanted to live. He went to New York in 1903 and, after the 1906 earthquake, to San Francisco. He became a labor contractor for many Spanish immigrants on farms in the Sacramento and San Joaquin valleys. He prospered since he knew English and Spanish dialects. At this point in his life he met Maria Rodriguez and a relationship began that led to marriage in San Francisco in 1911.

Maria was the daughter of Antonio Rodriguez and Carmen Sanchez Rodriguez and was born in 1894, in Salobrena, Provincia Granada, Spain. She left Malaga, Spain, in April 1907, traveling with her family on the steamer *Heliopolis* bound for Hawaii through the Strait of Magellan. The arduous voyage took about two months and the family was committed to work in Hawaii for at least two years. Maria's father had died when she was quite young and her mother had married a widower, Frank Cano, who had two children, Tony and Domingo.

The family was able to save enough money working in Hawaii to pay for passage to San Francisco in 1909. Maria found employment in a cigar factory there and she preferred it to working in the sugar cane fields of Hawaii. Her stepfather and brothers could not find work in San Francisco, however. So when the two Cano boys visited Santa Clara and found opportunities to work in a pleasant environment, the whole family moved to Santa Clara and made it their home.

When the Sapenas and Canos first came to Santa Clara, the city had many people who had come from

Italy, Spain, and Portugal. Many of these immigrants worked on farms and in canneries, saving money, buying homes, educating their children, venturing into various businesses and becoming pillars of the community. They did their own canning and butchering and made their own wine. All family members contributed: wives and mothers maintained the home, sewed and ensured that their children were well fed, clothed and trained in the beliefs of their church. So it was with Maria and Antonio.

Antonio and Maria's first home in Santa Clara was in the 1700 block of Benton Street near Pierce. Later they moved to 1735 Harrison Street. The couple had five children, all of whom attended Santa Clara schools. Antonio established a thriving business selling fish, pigs, grapes for wine, watermelons, fruit and whatever else he could provide. He often traveled as far away as Tracy by horse and wagon and later by truck to make sales on his established route. During the canning season he made his truck into a bus to take neighbors to and from work. During the Depression he operated a fruit stand at the corner of Clay and Lincoln streets, selling oranges, bananas and other fruit as well as soda pop and miscellaneous items. He bought grapes by the carload to sell to families to make wine.

In addition to tending to her own children and home, Maria worked for the John Fatjo family, among others. The children worked in the yard, raising chickens for eggs and meat. They were so successful that they sold their excess produce. The children also enjoyed pets which included dogs, cats and birds.

When the couple moved to Santa Clara, they became acquainted with Grace Steinhart, who lived in a lovely home at 1585 Fremont Street and who for many years conducted citizenship classes in the community. Antonio was already adept in the English language and Maria attended school at night to become fluent. Inspired by Steinhart and because of her interest in her adopted country, Maria encouraged many to gain fluency in English and secure their citizenship papers. During World War II, Maria raised money for the war effort, particularly for the USO and the Red Cross. She organized meetings at her home, but soon she and her patriotic friends became too numerous so it was necessary to move the meeting place to City Hall.

Maria and Antonio's oldest child, Anthony (Tony), was born in 1912. At age 20, he signed up as a volunteer with the fire department. During the war years he

Rodriquez and Cano family members. Rear: Carmen Rodriquez Cano and her husband Frank Cano. Front: Domingo Cano, Maria Rodriquez [Sapena], and Tony Cano. Courtesy Sapena family to the Austen Warburton Collection.

Hall was built.

Responsibilities of the marshal expanded over time and he hired nightwatchmen to walk the town's streets at night. One particularly popular watchman, George Whybark, was killed while investigating a prowler at a Franklin Street bar in 1910. By about this time, it also became necessary to draft traffic ordinances for horse-drawn carriages, bicycles, farm equipment and automobiles.

Beginning in 1921, George "Pete" Fallon served as Santa Clara's marshal. He convinced motorists and cyclists to conform to a speed limit by roaring up next to them on his motorcycle. Later he hired the first town traffic officers. During his tenure, communication between officer and headquarters was rather primitive as compared with today. Red lights stood along Franklin Street at The Alameda, Washington, and Lincoln streets. When a call came for help, the red lights would blaze, which called the officer back to the station to find out where the complaint was. At night, the police station was closed, so the local telephone operator dispatched all the calls. Just as Marshal Fallon got ready to retire, the police cars were outfitted with two-way radios. Fallon served until 1948, and was ever popular for being tough on violent crime but "looking the other way" in instances of bootlegging or bookmaking.

Just after the war, Frank Sapena was hired and in 1950 was promoted to "inspector" where he served until being elected chief of police in 1955.

was engaged in defense work and he married Ann Lacitignola in 1942. They had two sons, Anthony and David.

Tony pursued his interest in fire prevention, working in the fire department of the City of San José for 30 years and retiring as assistant fire chief in 1977. During his career he also was a member of the National Association of Fire Chiefs and he served on the boards of a number of organizations including Pacific Neighbors, Hope for Retarded Children and Adults, the California Pioneers of Santa Clara County, and the O'Connor Hospital 89ers, of which he was chairman 1976-77. He was appointed Honorary Fire Chief of San José, Costa Rica, in 1964 and was appointed to Santa Clara County's Committee on Mental Retardation in 1965. He was also a chairman of the Exchange Firemans Committee. In 1973 Tony and his brother Frank were recognized in the *San Jose Mercury News* as "top Hispano-Americans" in the field of public safety. Tony passed away in 1985 at the age of 73.

Antonio and Maria's second child, Carmen, was born in 1914. Even while attending school Carmen obtained a work permit when she was just twelve years of age. She worked for the Pratt-Low Cannery on Bellomy Street during school vacations. Upon completion of her schooling, she went to work for Pratt-Low full-time, and later for its successor Duffy Mott. At age 27, she was made a supervisor, although she protested, preferring to continue to do piece work. The boss, however, suggested that she should "help out for awhile as supervisor" and that "while" continued for 31 years. In the course of her 46 years of employment, machines replaced work that originally was done by hand. The plant closed in 1972, and Carmen went to work for Mayfair for 5 years. She retired at the age of 63 in order to help her ailing mother, Maria.

Antonio and Maria's third child, Frank, was born in 1916. As a youth, Frank was interested in hunting and fishing. He also enjoyed Golden Gloves boxing,

and was a two-time amateur boxing champion in 1933 and 1934. During World War II, he joined the Coast Guard and became captain of a gunnery department on an AKA ship and participated in the invasions of New Guinea, New Britain, the Admiralty Islands, and Hollandia, Dutch Guiana. While assisting with the beach landing at Dutch Guiana, the ship was torpedoed and Frank was one of 87 rescued by Army amphibious vehicles after four and half hours in the water. He was hospitalized for injuries for 11 months at a naval hospital in Pennsylvania. While Frank was hospitalized, he met Doris Brett and later the couple was married. Their children include Joe, Frank, Bruce, Shirley and Robert. Upon his release from service, he worked at Moffett Field and then decided to go into police work.

Frank joined the Santa Clara Police Department as a patrolman in December 1947 and moved up through the ranks, serving as a traffic officer in 1949, a detective in 1950, a juvenile officer in 1952, and as inspector of detectives in 1953. He took a leave of absence in 1955 to run for chief of police on an eight-point program to reform and improve the department. He was elected and re-elected, serving as chief for 20 of the 28 years of his service with the department. Frank attended Santa Clara University, the University of California School of Police Administration, the California Police Officers Administrative Institute, and San José City College Law Enforcement School. Under his administration the Police Department grew from 21 to 153 men and women. Frank initiated programs that included psychiatric examinations for patrolmen, a juvenile advisory counsel for first offenders, and vacation checks for residential homes. He also reorganized the department into three divisions: service, patrol and crime prevention. He established an Internal Affairs Bureau, a Vice and Narcotics Bureau, a Juvenile Bureau, participated in the construction of a new Police Administration Building, provided a new department training center, raised department standards, modernized training programs, and hired the department's first woman police officer.

He served on various boards of directors, including the Santa Clara Youth Village, YMCA, Disabled American War Veterans, Little League Baseball, Pop Warner Football, Seventh Step Foundation, United Fund Budget Committee, Rotary Club of Santa Clara, and American Legion Post 419, Santa Clara. He was awarded the title of Citizen of the Year in 1958 and again in 1963. He received the Exchange Club Community Service Award three years running, in 1965, 1966 and 1967. He served as president of the Santa Clara County Chiefs of Police and served on advisory boards at San José City College and West Valley College.

Frank's work with the department was the subject of a feature article in the December 1974 issue of *Guns and Ammo* magazine. Upon Frank's retirement as chief, in recognition of his achievements, the City of Santa Clara declared May 17, 1975 as "Frank Sapena Day." At a testimonial dinner that night at Santa Clara University, hundreds of friends gathered to pay tribute to his years of great service.

Frank's younger sister was Teresa Sapena, born in 1918. Upon completion of her schooling in the Santa Clara schools, Teresa worked in sales for several major department stores including Sears, Hales, and Macy's. During World War II, Teresa was an interpreter at a clinic in San José. Following the war, she met and married Frank Romero, who worked for Safeway for many years. The couple had one daughter, Cheryl, who married Robert O'Brien. In addition to her home activities and work, Teresa volunteered at O'Connor Hospital. Frank Romero died in 1981.

Antonio and Maria Sapena's youngest child, Joseph, was born in 1921. After completing his education in the Santa Clara schools, Joe began studies at San José State. When World War II began, he enlisted in the Navy as an aviation cadet. He reported to St. Mary's College, where the Navy Pre-Flight Training School was located. The trainees were instructed by noted athletes and coaches from all over the country, among them were Frankie Albert and Nello Falaschi. After St. Mary's College, Joe was sent to Los Alamitos N.A.S., where he received primary training, then Corpus Christi, Texas, for Basic and Advanced Flight Training where he was trained as a fighter pilot. When he received his flight wings, he worked as a test pilot for the Navy.

When Joe was released from the Navy, he enrolled at San José State for the completion of his studies. He was president of the Philosophy Club, appointed to the Spanish Honor Society, Sigma Delta Pi, and he earned the Outstanding Boxer Award. Upon graduation from San José State he went to the University of Chicago where he earned his master's degree.

Although Joe had opportunities to teach away from his home town, he wanted to return to Santa Clara. Upon returning he discovered that it was too late to apply for a college position. He went to see Emil Buchser, Sr., the school district superintendent, to discuss the local employment situation. Buchser offered him a job working in one of the schools and he remained with the district for almost 25 years. He also taught at West Valley College for seven years.

Joe and his wife Dora purchased a Taco Bell franchise. When the business began, Dora provided the management skill and Joe would work after school and weekends. They purchased additional franchises and in 1978 he took an early retirement to devote full time to the growing business. Joe and Dora had one daughter, Heidi.

The senior Sapenas continued to work in the community until their deaths. Antonio passed away in 1962 and Maria in 1979. All of the Sapena family members can look with pride at their accomplishments, which make them a significant chapter in the Santa Clara saga.

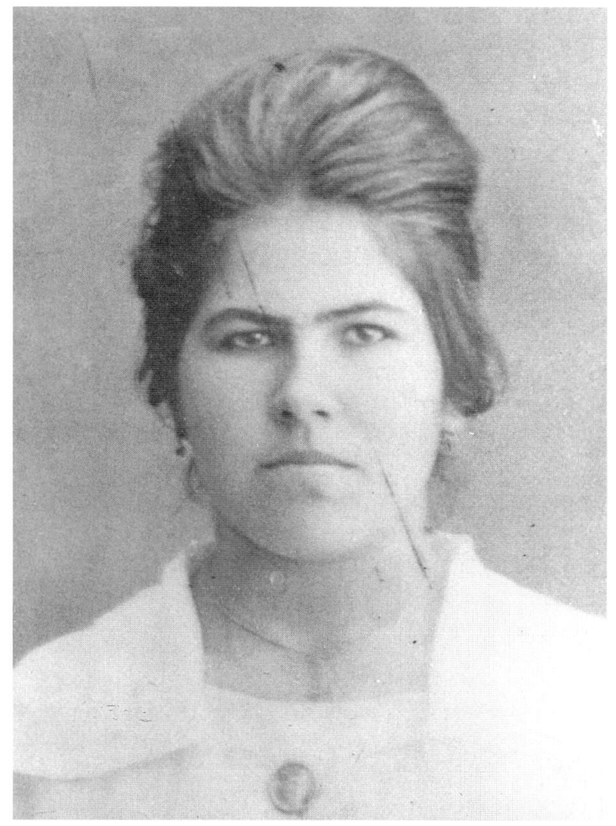

THE SANCHEZ AND CALLEJON FAMILIES

John and Josephine (Callejon) Sanchez established an outstanding family who have served the Santa Clara community. Their roots lie deep in the Province of Malaga on the south coast of Spain, known as the Costa Del Sol, the "sunny coast."

John's parents, Pablo Sanchez and Maria Trujillo, and their parents before them were farmers and Pablo's mother at one time owned and operated a large bakery in her hometown. Pablo's father sailed to the New World in the early 1800s and returned to Spain with tales of adventure and opportunity, tales that became part of the Sanchez family lore. So it was understandable that Pablo was interested when Don Carlos

Crovetto brought posters advertising opportunities in the New World and in Hawaii. The notices offered free passage to Hawaii and employment as agricultural workers, earning as much as twenty gold American dollars a month during the first year and twenty-one the second. Wives could work for twelve gold American dollars a month and children over 15 could earn fifteen. After three years, a family could get a house and an acre of land. What an opportunity!

John Sanchez was born in Malaga in 1898, and his sister Isabel, two years later. By the time John's parents saw the Crovetto notice, John had learned to read and write Spanish and his imagination had been stirred by his grandfather's tales of the New World. It was easy therefore, for the family to decide to go, and in 1907 they left Malaga on the British ship *Heliopolis*, bound for Hawaii through the Strait of Magellan.

After enduring a month of stormy seas, the crowded ship stopped for supplies and water at the world's southernmost town, Punta Arenas. There were no docking facilities, so water and supplies had to be brought to the ship by small boats. Some of the men were so frustrated and sick and tired of shipboard life that they literally jumped off the ship to be picked up by these boats, and remained in Punta Arenas.

With the additional supplies, the ship set sail into the Pacific and on to Hawaii, where Pablo and Maria Sanchez worked to fulfill their contract for passage. Though still a boy, John was so proficient in Spanish that a number of other families hired him to teach their children Spanish so that they might not lose their mother tongue. John's parents valued education and encouraged their children to read and to study. They kept up with events in Spain by means of a Spanish-language newspaper which was sent to Hawaii at infrequent intervals. Pablo also wanted his children to learn geography so he ordered a geography book to be shipped to them from far-away New York.

Not too long after their arrival, tragedy struck when Maria died on the island of Kauai. Pablo and the children moved to the island of Hawaii, near Hilo, where John and Isabel attended the local school. Pablo married Juana Rodriguez and remained in the Hilo area for about 10 years. During this time, both children attended school and became fluent in English as well as Spanish. Pablo saved his earnings and acquired property in Hawaii, providing his children with all the opportunities he could.

In 1918, Pablo Sanchez heard of better opportunities on the mainland and he moved his family to California and settled in Santa Clara. The home where they first lived still stands on Madison Street. At that time Madison was unpaved, as were most of the streets in Santa Clara. The Sanchez family shopped at the John Fatjo store on Franklin Street, where they found not only quality groceries but also good advice and credit from the tall and kind owner.

During the asparagus season, both Pablo and John worked for the Booth company near Sacramento, where John became a foreman. After asparagus season, John returned to Santa Clara and worked as a carpenter for Hiatt Construction Company, helping to build some of the homes on Hedding Street in San José. A number of those homes are still standing, attesting to the good workmanship! John also tended pear orchards for Sarah Winchester, a reclusive lady whose historic home stands on Winchester Boulevard in San José.

About this time, John became reacquainted with Josephine Callejon, whose family story followed a similar pattern to John's. Josephine's parents, Antonio and Maria Lopez Callejon, also had many centuries of history in the Malaga province of Spain. Her mother's father had a large farm in the province on which he produced all sorts of fruits and vegetables and raised livestock. They also saw the notice promulgated by Don Carlos Crovetto about opportunities in Hawaii. At that time Antonio and Maria Callejon had four children. The oldest, Josephine, was born in 1902. Her brother was James and her sisters were Catherine and Mary.

Attracted by greater opportunity, the family, which had been living in Estepona, travelled to Gibraltar in 1911 to board the Dutch ship *Willisdenn* for the trip across the Atlantic to the Strait of Magellan. This was the third ship of immigrants that Crovetto had arranged. Again the voyage was difficult and again some of the men jumped ship at Punta Arenas when the ship stopped for supplies. Surprisingly enough, the small boats bringing supplies from Punta Arenas carried some of the young men who had abandoned the *Heliopolis*, the ship on which the Sanchez family had come several years before. The men called to those on the ship, asking for news of their families in Spain.

First grade class, Fremont Elementary School, Santa Clara, 1947-48. Teacher seated on the right is Mary Gomez. Courtesy Mary Gomez to the Austen Warburton Collection.

was born there and, in memory of little Mary, was also named Mary. Josephine attended school near Hilo, where she met John Sanchez, another student there. Their friendship was interrupted, however, because Josephine's family moved to California in 1917, a year before John's.

The Callejons stayed in San Francisco for a brief time before taking up permanent residence in Santa Clara. Antonio Callejon worked in agriculture in the Santa Clara Valley. His children continued their education in local schools, except Josephine who, as the eldest, worked in the canneries.

John and Josephine, reacquainted and eventually betrothed, were married at Mission Santa Clara in 1921, with Father Raggio, S.J., officiating. The young couple rented a house on Pierce Street. They had two children: Mary born in 1922 and John born in 1924. John Sr. worked at the Rosenberg Brothers' packing house, near the railroad depot in Santa Clara. He was appointed foreman, and he continued working there for 27 years. When a better opportunity was offered him, he went to work for Sunsweet, where he also served as foreman until his retirement 15 years later in 1963. Josephine also worked at Rosenberg Brothers for 26 years, and when that company went out of business, she went to work for Mayfair Packing Company until her retirement in 1965.

Both John and Josephine believed in working and saving, and they encouraged their children to get the best education possible. The two children attended Santa Clara schools and graduated from Santa Clara High School. Mary was determined to become a teacher and graduated from San José State College with her teacher's certificate in 1943. Mary first taught at King City, then at old McKinley School in Sunnyvale. In 1946, she came back to Santa Clara and began her 34-year tenure as one of the Santa Clara school system's outstanding teachers. Her classes included the first and second grades at the lovely old Spanish-style Fremont

A measles epidemic broke out en route to Hawaii particularly affecting the children, including little Mary, who was about three years of age. The ship's officers put all those afflicted into quarantine, and Maria Callejon, Mary's mother, volunteered to serve as their nurse and cook. She had to spend the rest of the voyage in isolation. The authorities in Hawaii continued the quarantine until the affected part of the ship could be thoroughly cleaned. Little Mary, however, never recovered and died shortly after arriving in the islands.

The Callejon family lived near Hilo for about five years, working in the sugar cane fields. Another child

School, the second grade at Washington School, and the second grade at Scott Lane School. Reading was one of her favorite subjects and as a teacher she touched the lives of dozens and dozens of Santa Clara children. Among her noted students were Ed Sousa, later mayor of the city, Kirby Shaw, who became a doctor of music, and Ricky Strini, a noted glass artist.

In 1943, the day after her graduation from college, Mary married James Gomez, a member of another prominent Santa Clara family. The wedding took place during a leave from James' service with the U.S. Coast Guard. Mary and James have one child, Mary Michele Barovsky, born in 1953.

Mary Sanchez Gomez was active in other aspects of the community besides education. She participated in the development of a parks and recreation department and served on its first commission, which formulated the city's policy to have a park in every neighborhood. In appreciation of her efforts, the city named Mary Gomez Park after her. Mary also held memberships in the Santa Clara Woman's Club, Delta Kappa Gamma (an international honor society for educators), the California Teachers' Association, the National Education Association, Santa Clara Cultural Society, O'Connor 89ers, the Triton Museum, and many other organizations. She has also served for a number of years on the youth advisory committee of the Santa Clara Police Department. Mary was named outstanding teacher of the year for the Santa Clara Unified School District in 1972.

John Sanchez, the second child of John and Josephine, graduated from Santa Clara High School in 1943, entered the Army, and served in the Aleutian Islands as a staff sergeant. After more than three years of service and numerous decorations, John returned to Santa Clara to attend San José State. He went to work for the U.S. Post Office as a mail carrier and 20 years later, in 1967, became Santa Clara's postmaster, a position he held for 18 years. He helped develop a postal

program for the community as it grew from a small town into a large city.

Besides being postmaster, John served for 11 years on the Postmaster's Selection Board for the Pacific Area, encompassing the 13 Western states and the Pacific islands. John was noted for his sense of humor and, called on frequently to speak at functions, he was occasionally teased about his small stature. Someone might call out: "Hey Sanchez, we can hear you but we can't see you!" His typical response would be to climb on a chair and shout back: "Now you can see all of me!" In 1981 when John learned he was afflicted with a serious disease and underwent a series of operations, he told his doctor, "Doctor, you take care of me and I'll take care of your mail."

(Opposite page) Poster circulated in Spain by Don Carlos Crovetto to encourage emigration. Courtesy Mary Gomez to the Austen Warburton Collection.

John Sanchez, Santa Clara Postmaster from 1967 to 1984. Courtesy Mary Gomez to the Austen Warburton Collection.

EMIGRACION CON PASAJE GRATUITO AL ESTADO
DE HAWAI,
(ESTADOS-UNIDOS DE AMÉRICA)
Descripción de las Islas Haway, según el célebre viajero M. C. de Variony

...Es punto menos que imposible hacer comprender, á quien no los ha disfrutado, los incomparables atractivos del clima de las Islas de Hawai. Una temperatura constantemente igual, que todo lo mas varia diez grados, y que casisiempre está á 30° centígrados; un cielo purísimo, apenas velado de vez en cuando por frescas nubecillas y lluvias oportunas; una naturaleza alegre y lozana, admirablemente iluminada por un sol radiante, constituyen el atractivo mas poderoso para atraer al extranjero y obligarle á prolongar su permanencia en aquellas Islas. Las tempestades son muy raras allí, tan raras como los huracanes, que suelen ser el azote de los paises intertropicales; las noches, sobre todo, son sumamente apacibles, y cuando brilla la luna, envolviendo las campiñas en los suaves y misteriosos efluvios de sus rayos, cualquera se creería víctima de una ilusión encantadora. Es tan pura y despejada la atmósfera que á media noche se puede leer á la claridad combinada de la luz y las estrellas. En ninguna parte se extiende la vía láctea con tanto explendor y majestad como allí: las constelaciones invisibles en Europa, iluminan el espacio y brillan como deslumbradoras perlas: el mar despliega en la costa sus oleadas fosforescentes y mece sus plácidos ensueños con lento y monótono movimiento...

Los emigrantes Españoles que quieran acojerse á las concesiones y beneficios que ofrecen las Leyes de Inmigración y Colonización del Estado de HAWAI, obtienen pasage gratuito desde Málaga para dicho Estado, en magníficos Vapores de marcha rápida, de más de 12.000 toneladas, con comida, durante el viaje, á la Española, condimentada por cocineros embarcados expresamente para ello.

El Gobierno de dicho Estados, bajo cuya garantía se efectúa la emigración, ofrece, á los VERDADEROS AGRICULTORES un porvenir halagüeño, cuyas ventajas son las siguientes:

Los varones cabeza de familia

20 duros americanos oro, al mes, durante el primer año de trabajo.

21 duros americanos oro, al mes, durante el segundo año.

22 duros americanos oro, al mes, durante el tercer año.

Las mujeres, sus esposas 12 duros oro al mes.

Los demás individuos de su familia que sean mayores de 15 años, 15 duros mensuales, si son varones y 10 duros si son hembras.

Desde que desembarquen, se les facilita una magnífica casa-vivienda (que vale más de 500 pesos oro) agua y lumbre y escuela gratuita, donde reciben educación los hijos menores, para los que es obligatorio asistir á ella.

Y á los **tres años** de trabajo, con buena conducta y en los que hayan demostrado que son buenos Labradores (y especialmente para el cultivo de la caña de azúcar), se les cede gratuitamente y en propiedad absoluta y sin gravámen alguno, la casa donde esten viviendo y además una fanega de tierra.

Condiciones que deben reunir los emigrantes

Es condición indispensable que los emigrantes sean **agricultores** que gozen de buena salud, no padezcan de la vista, que no tengan defectos físicos y que formen precisamente **familias** cuya constitución puede ser, como sigue:

1.º Marido y mujer sin hijos, no teniendo el marido **más de 45 años**, ni la mujer **más de 40**.

2.º Marido y mujer con hijos, no pudiendo los jefes tener más de **45** años, con tal que haya en la familia un hombre útil **de 17 á 45 años.**

3.º Viudo ó viuda con hijos, teniendo siempre un hombre útil **mayor de 17 años y menor de 45 años.**

4.º Hombre casado no llevando la mujer, pero si llevando hijos con tal que haya siempre un hombre útil de **17 á 45 años.**

5.º Mujer casada no llevando su marido, pero si llevando hijos con tal que haya uno útil de **17 á 45 años.**

Podrán ir como agregados á las familias antes expresadas, todos los parientes, carnales y políticos, menores de 40 años.

Las personas mayores de 45 años no gozan de pasaje gratuito: estas tienen que pagarse el pasaje que cuesta Pesetas 400.

Documentos que necesitan presentar las familias que deseen emigrar

1.º Cédula personal para todos los mayores de 14 años.

2.º Los varones y mujeres solteras, hasta la edad de 23 años, una autorización de sus padres ó tutores, otorgada ante Notario ó ante el Alcalde del pueblo de su vecindad. Este documento no es necesario cuando vayan en compañía de sus padres, pero en todo caso las mujeres solteras han de presentar un certificado que acredite su estado de soltería.

3.º Partida de bautismo para todos los varones y mujeres solteros.

4.º Los varones de 15 á 20 años no pueden embarcar sin presentar un certificado que acredite haber consignado en la Caja de Depósito la suma de 1.500 pesetas á las resultas de la quinta, según previene la ley.

5.º Los varones de 20 á 40 años han de presentar la licencia absoluta si son licenciados definitivos. Los que pertenezcan á la reserva ó á la clase de reclutas disponibles han de presentar un permiso del Capitán General del distrito respectivo, autorizándoles para efectuar su embarque ó ausentarse de la Península. Este documento no puede tener más de 4 meses á contarse desde la fecha de su expedición.

6.º Las mujeres casadas que no vayan acompañadas de sus maridos han de presentar un permiso de éste, visado por la Alcaldía del pueblo de su vecindad ó por Notario, siendo en la Capital.

7.º Partida de casamiento para los matrimonios.

8.º Partida de viudedad para las viudas.

9.º Certificado de buena conducta expedido por la Alcaldía de su residencia con las señas personales, para todos los indivíduos mayores de 14 años.

10 Certificado de no estar procesado, expedido por el Juzgado del pueblo donde residan, para todos los mayores de 14 años, ó de la Audiencia siendo en la Capital.

DESCONFIAR DE LOS INTERMEDIARIOS
Para mayores detalles y presentación de documentos:
DON CARLOS CROVETTO, Encargado del Departamento de Revisión
CALLE DE RIOS ROSAS (antes Cañón) núm. 3.--Málaga

John was a member of the Native Sons of the Golden West and served as a volunteer fireman for 25 years as a member of the Tanner Hose Company. His interests included service with the Red Cross, the Boys Scouts of America, the United Way, and the Crippled Children's Society. When the city of Santa Clara produced a film on the story of the community in 1976 for the nation's bicentennial, John was active in planning the program and played the role of Father de la Peña, the Franciscan priest who founded Mission Santa Clara.

John Sanchez married Rita Arnold in 1947. They had two children: John born in 1953, and Peter born in 1961. John went into the military and became a member of the Special Forces (Green Beret) Unit of the U.S. Army. A career military man, he served as a master sergeant based at Fort Lewis, Washington. Peter attended Santa Clara schools and graduated from Mitty High School in San José. He worked for the Pepsi Cola Company.

Upon retirement, John and Josephine Sanchez were able to look back on lives of great achievement. With their encouragement, help, and inspiration, their children became two outstanding citizens of Santa Clara. John and Josephine lived in their family home on Lafayette Street for 46 years, watching as the dirt street changed to concrete and the horse-drawn water wagon was replaced by fancy street sweepers. The changing pace of traffic complicated life to the point where they no longer considered it safe to use their driveway.

John Sanchez, Jr., the beloved postmaster of Santa Clara, died in 1984. His father, John Sanchez, Sr., died in 1985.

As is the case with many of the families from Spain, John and Josephine Sanchez found Santa Clara was home to some of their sisters, nieces, nephews, and other relatives. Among these are several other local families such as Catherine Callejon Toledo, Josephine's sister who accompanied her from Gibralter to the

Hawaiian Islands in 1911. She was married to Anthony R. Toledo, former mayor of Santa Clara. Their brother James' son is Don Callejon, who served the children of this community for many years, retiring in 1990 as superintendent of the Santa Clara Unified School District. Josephine's other sister, Mary Hidalgo, also attended Santa Clara schools.

The Ruiz and Menacho Families

Mary Ruiz (Menacho) was born in Loja, Granada, Spain, in 1910. Her father, Julian Ruiz, raised vegetables for local markets and married Amalia Olid whose parents were sheepherders. The couple had five children while in Spain: Vince, Dolores, Mary, Amalia and Julian. Little Amalia died of scarlet fever.

Hearing of opportunities in Hawaii, the family left Loja, Granada, in 1913 aboard the English ship *Escort*. Sailing with many other immigrants similarly bound for a new life, the trip around Cape Horn took 63 long days. During the voyage, cramped passengers suffered from a measles epidemic and severe malnutrition which led to the death of Mary's one-year old brother, Julian, whose little body was buried at sea. Julian's aunt and uncle, Felicidad and Fernando Cruz, and their three boys, Joseph, Fernando, and Enrique, were also aboard the ship.

In Maui, Hawaii, Julian worked for about six years in the sugar cane fields, being paid in gold at the outset at the rate of $20 per month. Family members still cherish one of the original $20 gold pieces earned by Julian. Two more sons were born to the family in Hawaii: Manuel, who died during another measles epidemic, and Tony, who moved with the rest of the family to Santa Clara in 1919.

Thirteen members of the Ruiz and Cruz families lived in a small home at 870 Fremont Street in Santa Clara. At that time it was still a dirt street and there was no electricity in the home. They did have the convenience of a flush toilet, although it was located outside

Dedication of Saint Clare's Church, 1926. Courtesy Santa Clara University Archives.

the house. During the influenza epidemic of 1919, the whole family became sick, and little Tony and Fernando Cruz, Sr., died from it.

The first job that Julian had in Santa Clara was thinning fruit in a nearby apricot orchard. The whole family picked prunes at the large orchard owned by the Butcher family which was known as Butcher's Corner. They were paid by the ton.

Mary attended the old red brick Intermediate School and graduated in 1926. In order to contribute to the family income, she took a job at the Pratt-Low Cannery on Bellomy Street, working with various fruit products, especially peaches. In 1930, she went to Monterey in search of work cutting and packing in the

Pratt-Low fruit processors, Santa Clara and Redwood City plants. Courtesy Bea Lichtenstein Collection.

fish canneries. During the asparagus season she worked in the Sacramento area. Mary explained, "We picked peas, onions, sugar beets and whatever else we could find whenever and wherever there was work."

Eventually, the Ruiz family purchased property and rented out an apartment to a young couple. The young man's brother was Luis Menacho, and when he came to visit, he met Mary Ruiz. Three years later they were married by Father Raggio at St. Clare's Church.

Although they had never met, the Ruiz and Menacho families had migrated to Hawaii aboard the same ship, *Escort*, in 1913. Luis Menacho was eleven years of age when he left Cadiz, Spain, with his father, Atanacio, and his mother, Maria Morales-Menacho. There were eight children in his family, including Frank, Joe, Luis, John, Manuel, Josephine, Mary and Antoinette. Like Julian Ruiz, Atanacio had been a farmer in Spain, worked in the cane fields in Hawaii and later moved his family to Santa Clara to work in the orchards.

Luis Menacho was employed for 27 years as a sash man at Pacific Manufacturing Company on The Alameda in Santa Clara. He and Mary worked and saved and entered a partnership with his brother to purchase a Sunnyvale grocery store and a beer parlor. Twelve years later they sold the store and acquired the "Cork & Bottle" liquor store, which they operated for nine years.

Luis and Mary's children included Luis, Manuel, and Betty. Luis married Nancy Daniliff, had three children, and was employed as a special union representative for Local 428. Manuel married Joanne Moore, had four children, and worked in inventory control. Betty was a teacher at the Wilcox School.

After suffering a stroke, Luis retired and sold the liquor store business, and he died in 1977. Mary was employed by the Santa Clara Unified School District in the food services department and eventually the old Fremont Street house was sold to make way for ten condominiums.

CHAPTER SIX

CULTURE

LASS, POGUE, RHODE AND KULPA

Warburton exhibits his concern for and interest in the arts, education, heritage and other cultural causes in Santa Clara and beyond. He discusses descendants of a sea captain whose home became an historical museum, a teacher, a whole family of artists, and a public relations expert who promoted local arts and history groups. From the voluminous correspondence between Airi Kulpa and Austen Warburton that is part of the author's research material, it is obvious they were close personal friends and shared many interests, particularly related to Santa Clara.

THE LASS FAMILY

The handsome two-story Italianate Victorian house at 1889 Market Street in Santa Clara was the home of Captain Christian S. Lass, a German-born sailing-ship owner and master, and early prune rancher. Today the building is the Harris-Lass Historical Museum.

Christian S. Lass was born in 1843, in the German province of Schleswig, the eldest of five children of Frederick and Johanna Brock Lass. He went to sea as a cabin boy when he was 15, eventually arriving in San Francisco in 1862 as an able seaman. During the Civil War, he sailed the sloop *General Brady* for the Union government. By 1868, Lass became master of the schooner *Annie Forbes* on the Sacramento River. In 1873, he bought the two-year old *Elnorah*, and he commanded that vessel until 1885, engaged principally in trade in the Pacific Basin, with frequent voyages to Mexico and Hawaii.

In 1886, with two partners, Lass built a three-masted schooner, *The Comet*, which had a capacity of 429 tons. This substantial vessel was built in the shipyards at Fort Blakeley, Washington, and was used not only in the Pacific Coast trade but also on voyages as far as Australia. The Captain's favorite vessel, however, was built under his supervision in 1891, also at Fort Blakeley. *The Meteor* was a four-masted schooner, 177 feet long with a beam of 38 feet and a displacement of

The Harris-Lass house, purchased by the city in 1987, is currently an historical museum operated by the Historic Preservation Society of Santa Clara. Photograph by the author.

518 tons. Captain Lass sailed her only until 1895 when a shipboard fall injured his spine and forced him to retire. During the course of his life, Captain Lass purchased interests in some 18 ships but he always considered *The Meteor* his flagship. She sailed on until 1923, one of the last of the Pacific sailing ships. Her last voyage was in the sugar trade between the Hawaiian Islands and Port Townsend in Washington state. Later

A 19th-century carriage, housed in the adjacent barn. Photograph by the author.

she was shorn of her masts and converted into an Alaskan fish packer. A painting of the ship in her glory days still hangs in the living room of the Harris-Lass Historical Museum.

Captain Lass made San Francisco his home port during his years at sea, living in a house atop Telegraph Hill. In 1869, he married Julia Anna Christina Peterson Jorgenson, who had been born in Hamburg. The couple had two children: Frederick and Henry. The latter, following in his father's footsteps, became master of the schooner *John Campbell*, engaged in Pacific Coast trade. Later he commanded a passenger steamer plying between San Pedro and Catalina Island.

In 1894 Captain Lass purchased 38 acres in Santa Clara, between today's Bellomy and Newhall streets. Shortly after purchasing the property, he erected a two-story residence where he continued to live until 1906, when he moved to the Market Street home. The captain's son Frederick operated the prune ranch on the 38

A painting of Captain Lass's flagship, the Meteor, *hangs in the Harris-Lass house. Photograph by the author.*

acres and he and his wife Julia Wilhelmina, whom he married in 1897, lived there with his parents. Frederick and Julia had three daughters: Carolina Fredericka, born in 1898, Julia Louisa, born the next year, and Johanna Caroline, born in 1901.

The granddaughters of Captain Lass had many memories of life on the ranch with the captain. He was a strict disciplinarian and an elbow on the dining table was met with the command, "Go get a block of wood." The wood was then applied to the erring elbow to impress on a young mind the importance of table manners.

Household supplies were bought in quantities suitable for a long sea voyage, with coffee beans, flour, sugar and soap laid in by the hundred pounds, oil and syrup by the gallons and canned foods by the dozens. A green stalk of bananas was put in the cellar while another was on the back porch ripening and yet a third, this one ripe, was in the pantry ready for use. Beans were always on the Saturday breakfast table, because beans had always been served on the captain's vessels on Saturday morning. In loading a buggy or automobile, the captain carefully calculated the weight of both cargo and passengers, taking care to distribute it evenly, just as

THE DAY THE PRESIDENT CAME TO TOWN

In May of 1903, President Theodore Roosevelt visited California, and made a special point of stopping at Santa Clara. He had given a "manly" speech at the San José rail depot, and then his entourage made its way down The Alameda to Mission Santa Clara. The President was greeted by hundreds of townspeople and Santa Clara University students as their student band played "Hail Columbia."

The President stood in his carriage and "gazed admiringly" at the attractive campus huddled around the Mission, while the church bells pealed their welcome. The school's president, Father Robert Kenna warmly greeted the visiting Chief Executive. Kenna, like Roosevelt, was an ardent conservationist and had lent rigorous support to saving Big Basin, an ancient redwood grove in the Santa Cruz Mountains which was slated for the lumber mill. Two years earlier Kenna had pleaded with the California State Senate to save the redwoods:

I do not come to speak to you as a priest, nor as the president of a great college, nor in the language of such, but as a forty-niner, and in the language of one who loves the great land of the West and her magnificent forests, which so often charmed my boyhood days and thrilled my young heart with high and noble aspirations.

These redwoods are pre-eminently

Kenna's speech convinced reluctant senators to establish California's first state park, Big Basin. Roosevelt's own conservationist bent found a strong ally in Kenna.

Roosevelt gave a "vigorous address" at Santa Clara University, then his group made their way south, along Santa Clara-Los Gatos Road, today's Winchester Boulevard.

Interior furnishings of the Harris-Lass house include a number of antiques. These pieces are found in the sitting room. Johanna Lass, the last owner of the house, donated many of the original furnishings and farm equipment. Photographs by the author.

he had done so many times readying a vessel for sea.

During Theodore Roosevelt's presidency, the chief executive visited Santa Clara, and the Lass family proudly displayed their Victrola, one of the first in the valley, on the front porch as the President rode by. The captain was particularly interested in dahlias, and there were some 1,000 plants of 126 varieties in the garden surrounding the Lass home.

Shortly after the 1906 earthquake, the Lass property was sold to allow for expansion of the Catholic cemetery, and the house was used for many years as the home of the cemetery superintendent. Captain Lass and his family moved to the handsome two-story Victorian on Market Street. The 13-room house had an attic, a basement and had been built around 1865 by Henry Harris, later occupied by his son Albert Harris, founder of the Santa Clara Valley Bank. A massive safe is still in the basement of the house, one that Albert Harris used to safeguard cash and securities he often brought home after working late in the evening when the bank's vault had been closed. Albert Harris attended the College of the Pacific and served on the Santa Clara School Board

for 13 years. He was also a town trustee for two years.

The captain's wife, Julia Anna, died in 1910 and Captain Lass died ten years later in 1920 at the age of 76. He was buried in the Santa Clara cemetery, but his remains were later transferred to the family crypt at Oak Hill Cemetery in San José.

Frederick and Julia Wilhelmina continued to live in the Market Street house until their deaths in 1932 and 1969, respectively. The second daughter of Frederick and Julia Lass, Julia Louise, died at the age of 13 in Santa Clara. Johanna Caroline Lass, the youngest daughter, attended the College of the Pacific in San José, and in 1922 married Elwood William Haynes. Their only child, Elwood Jr., died in San Francisco at the age of 14. After her husband's death in 1955, Johanna spent much of her time at the Market Street house, where her mother and aunt and uncle lived. Her mother died in 1969 and Johanna moved again into the great house that her grandfather, Captain Christian Lass, had established as the family home more than sixty years before.

Frederick and Julia's eldest daughter, Carolina, married Thomas Walter Bull in 1918. She was active in civic affairs and served as a handicrafts judge for many years at the Santa Clara County Fair. Thomas worked as an electrician and automobile mechanic, but a venture into prune ranching in Sunnyvale failed during the Depression. There were four Bull children: Julia Elizabeth (b. 1922), Carolina Lass (b. 1924), Thomas Walter, Jr. (b. 1925), and Dorothy Jean (b. 1930).

The old sea captain and his descendants played an important role in the Santa Clara saga.

THE POGUE FAMILY

Jane Knox Pogue was born in Waimea, Kauai, Hawaii, in 1849. Known to members of the Pogue family as "Aunt Jennie," she was educated in Hawaii and taught at the Maunaolu Seminary on the island of Maui. She and the other Pogues who came to reside in Santa Clara had deep roots in Hawaii.

Her father, the Reverend John Fawcett Pogue, served as a missionary for the Congregational Church to Hawaii, arriving July 15, 1844, on the brig *Globe* after a voyage of 244 days from Boston, Massachusetts. He married Maria Kapule Whitney, the first Caucasian girl born in the Hawaiian islands. Pogue served not only as a missionary but also as an educator for many years. He was one of three men who received a grant of land of approximately 3,000 acres from King Kalakaua as a reward for services to the Hawaiian people. Pogue later sold his share of the property to Soreno Bishop, one of the other men who had received a grant, for $700.

The Pogues had four children, Elizabeth, Jane (Aunt Jennie), Samuel and William Fawcett. William married Emma Victoria Saffery in 1880. Emma was half Hawaiian and a descendant of the Hawaiian royal family.

Maria Kapule Whitney Pogue moved to California after the death of her husband. The family first settled in Napa and then moved to Santa Clara, where Maria lived with three of her children, Elizabeth, Jane and Samuel. The eight-acre ranch in Santa Clara on the Santa Clara-Los Gatos Road (today's Winchester

Pogue sisters, 1925. (L. to R.) Maria, Jennie, Frances, and Ruth. Courtesy Jennie Pogue Jepson to the Austen Warburton Collection.

Boulevard) opposite the Catholic cemetery was purchased in 1895 for a $10 gold piece. Maria died in Santa Clara April 20, 1900, and is buried with her husband at Oak Hill Cemetery in San José in the Pogue family plot. Aunt Jennie never married but helped to raise ten of her brother William's 14 children, who were born in Hawaii but sent to California to be educated.

A twelve-room Victorian home was erected on the Pogue ranch in 1896 to accommodate the large family. One by one, William Pogue's children came from Hawaii to live on the ranch while obtaining their educa-

Jennie Pogue (Jepson's) first car, a 1926 Star Coupster which cost $1,000. Courtesy Jennie Pogue Jepson to the Austen Warburton Collection.

The Pogue house across from the Catholic Cemetery on today's Winchester Boulevard built in 1896 and razed in the 1950s. Christmas card from Ruth Pogue to Austen Warburton, 1956.

tion in the Santa Clara schools. Edmund arrived in 1888 and later graduated from Santa Clara High School. William Fawcett Pogue, Jr., or "Willie" as he was called, also came to Santa Clara in 1888 and after graduating from the schools in Santa Clara went to Eureka to work in the lumber industry. Later he returned to the Santa Clara Valley and went into farming and construction work, working for a time for the Morrison Brothers Builders.

Another son, John Fawcett Pogue, arrived in Santa Clara in 1889 and, after he finished school, worked at various occupations including photographer, carpenter, printer, farmer, and gardener. During his life, he main-

tained the ranch property. He passed away in 1952 and is buried at Oak Hill Cemetery. Harvey Whitney Pogue came to Santa Clara in 1890 and became a professional musician. He was an accomplished violinist and directed an orchestra of his own in New York for many years. He supplied the Hawaiian orchestra at the 1915 Panama-Pacific International Exposition in San Francisco.

Coville Cory Pogue attended Santa Clara schools beginning in 1895. Upon graduation he worked for a time in a cattle ranch in Calexico, later returning to Maui to work on his father's cattle ranch. Maria Emma Pogue arrived in Santa Clara in 1897 and after graduating from the local schools attended the Kings Conservatory of Music and became an accomplished pianist. She married Edmund Pickett on February 4, 1918 at Aunt Jennie's house in Santa Clara, and moved with her husband to Oakland.

Charles Alexander Pogue came to California in 1901. He attended Santa Clara schools and Heald's Business College in San José. He was employed for a time as a teacher but continued with his education to become a certified public accountant. Ruth Elizabeth Pogue graduated from the Santa Clara schools in 1916. She continued to live with Aunt Jennie and upon the death of her aunt inherited the family ranch. Ruth was active in the Santa Clara Chapter of Eastern Star for 25 years, participated in Red Cross work during World War II, and was a well known musician, having studied at the Kings Conservatory of Music.

Henry Baldwin Pogue came to Santa Clara in 1920. After high school, he attended the University of California Davis, graduating in animal husbandry. He returned to Hawaii to work for his father and later moved to Fresno to become milk production manager for the Borden Company. Frances Victoria Pogue, the youngest of the William Pogue children to come to Santa Clara, arrived in California with her sister Jennie Pauahi Pogue in 1909. Jennie was about four years of age and Frances two. The two sisters were inseparable while living with Aunt Jennie. Frances graduated from Santa Clara High School in 1925 and studied nursing for a time at San José Hospital. In 1929 she married Harold Relph with whom she had two sons, James Edwin and Richard Harold.

Perhaps the best known of the Pogue children to be educated in Santa Clara was Jennie Pauahi Pogue, born Thanksgiving Day, November 30, 1905, in Kailua, Maui. Although her mother was forewarned of the coming birth early in the morning, she insisted on serving Thanksgiving dinner to family and guests. After serving the meal, she and her dedicated Japanese servant Momo, retired to her bedroom for the birth of Jennie, newest member of the Pogue clan.

Jennie was named for the Hawaiian princess Pauahi, the great grandchild of King Kamehameha. Pauahi's grandfather was Kaoleioka, one of the greatest of Hawaii's warrior kings. Pauahi met Charles Reed Bishop, an American, and later married him in New York. With the combination of Bishop wealth and royal Hawaiian lands they established the first Kamehameha School for Boys. Perhaps inspired by Princess Pauahi's interest in education, Jennie decided to become a teacher.

Jennie suffered a lifelong sadness because her parents sent her away as they did most of their children, to be raised by her maiden aunt in Santa Clara. She never saw her mother again. She recalled the sea voyage from Hawaii with the long deck of the ship and hot chocolate at bedtime. She remembered the sad party when she kissed her mother good-bye. Many nights in Santa Clara she would awaken from a dream thinking that her parents were at the front door ringing the bell. She would run down the flight of stairs but, finding no one there, would climb back up and cry herself to sleep.

Her Aunt Jennie's home was a large two-story building with five bedrooms and bath upstairs, one bedroom and a bath downstairs together with a parlor, liv-

Miss Jennie Pogue's (left) fifth grade class in Santa Clara in 1927-28. The man standing on the right is Mr. Wemay. Seated in the front row, second from the right is Austen Warburton. Courtesy Jennie Pogue Jepson to the Austen Warburton Collection.

ing room, dining room, kitchen and pantry. A huge basement was always filled to capacity with home canned food and all kinds of other items that gravitated to the home of the maiden aunt. Jennie's bedroom was upstairs and, since they had only coal-oil lamps, Jennie dreaded climbing the stairs and going into the darkness at bedtime. Jennie recalled,

> *My aunt had high ideals, and believe me, she instilled them into me. I had a genuine Puritanical bringing up which proved very fruitful during many temptations in my life. If I grew up to be half as good as she was, I can be happy. She was loved and known as Auntie Pogue to the whole town of Santa Clara. As she grew older she broadened her Puritanical rules, even permitting me and my sister*

"*Depression Babies,*" *1932, Jennie's son (third from right) and children of her friends. (L. to R.) Rudy Buchser, Jean Jensen, Jerry Sharp, Donald Jepson, Marjorie Higdon, and Marilyn Holmes. Courtesy Jennie Pogue Jepson to the Austen Warburton Collection.*

Maria's husband to play cards on Sunday. As a child I was not allowed to play with my dolls on Sunday—a day of real rest.

The aunt passed away in 1932 at her home in Santa Clara and was buried in the family plot at Oak Hill Cemetery.

Jennie reminisced about many of her teachers in the Santa Clara school system, beginning with Miss Applegaith and Miss Hayward, her first grade teachers. Other memorable teachers were Miss Roll for English, Miss Warren for art, Miss Graham for reading, Miss Gallimore for arithmetic and her beautiful music teacher, Miss Sanders, who wore the most attractive clothes and was such a "gallant lady." Jennie said that she always wanted to grow up to be equally as lovely a lady! Upon graduation from grammar school, the eighth graders made their own graduation dresses under the guidance of Miss Steinhart.

Her high school years in Santa Clara were happy years, with Mr. Townsend as principal at the two-story brick building which was later used to house the intermediate school. Miss Winchell was the English teacher and coach of the senior play. Miss Coeke, the Spanish teacher, spoke no English in the classroom and was dearly loved by all the students. On senior sneak day the entire class had a picnic and swim at Santa Cruz. Jennie's class was the first senior class to graduate from the new high school on Jackson Street in June 1923. This lovely red brick building was later demolished to make way for the new school now being used.

Jennie attended San José State College, traveling by street car from Santa Clara to the San José campus. Upon graduation in 1925, Jennie taught at Atwater Grammar School in Merced County where she earned $1,000 a year, teaching third, fourth and fifth grades. In 1926 she heard of the death of her mother in Hawaii and sadly looked back upon the last time she had seen her 17 years before.

In that same year Jennie applied for a position in the Santa Clara school system to teach in the sixth, seventh and eighth grades of the intermediate school where Emil Buchser was the principal. The year was memorable for Jennie for another reason. She purchased her first automobile, a Star Coupster which cost $1,000!

In 1927 Jennie took her first vacation to the Hawaiian islands to visit her father. Upon her return, she was transferred to Fremont School in Santa Clara and given a class of fifth graders. She never forgot the stimulating effect of this class which included students who later became famous in the Santa Clara Valley. These included Albert Giannini who eventually was a prominent surgeon, Marcus Lundin became a famous scientist, Wilda Mae Merritt was a renowned audiologist and head of that department at Franklin Hospital in San Francisco, Austen Warburton became an attorney and civic leader, and many other successful students. One day the principal called Jennie out of the classroom, and when she came back the children showered her with peanuts. They had been studying peanuts to learn how and where they were grown. Jennie did not know at first whether this episode was in fun or an angry bombardment. Actually it demonstrated the stu-dents' love for her and afterwards everyone had a good time feasting on the peanuts.

About the same time she was introduced to a farmer named George Jepsen. Emil Buchser, the principal, told her that George was "dying" to meet her. Buchser had also told George that Jennie was a "little teacher" who was "dying" to meet him! Romance blossomed and on July 20, 1928, Jennie became the bride of George Jepsen at her Aunt Jennie's house in Santa Clara. Jennie's sister Frances was the maid of honor and John Jepsen was the best man. In 1931, they had a son, Donald George Jepsen. He too was educated in the early years by Mrs. Gibson, Miss Linderoth, and Miss Berry. Eventually Don attended U.C. Davis and later Cal Poly.

Married women could not teach in the Santa Clara school system and Jennie was not rehired in 1928. During World War II, however, the rules were changed, and she was again hired to teach. After 30 years of teaching, Jennie retired. George Jepson died in 1953. Jennie was an active member of many volunteer groups including the Family Service Auxiliary, the YWCA, the Plunkett Plunkers Ukulele Club, the Soroptimist Club, the Retired Teachers' Club and many other organizations. Her activities included working with church groups at the Santa Clara Presbyterian Church where she served as an elder, a Sunday school teacher and president of the Women's Association. Eventually, the call of her native Hawaii became so strong that she returned to live in the land of her ancestors but remained in close contact with the many Santa Clarans who had been touched by her life.

The eight-acre ranch purchased in 1895 remained in the ownership of the Pogue family until it was acquired by developer David D. Bohannon for inclusion in the Westwood subdivision in the 1950s. Reportedly $32,000 was paid for the property. Ruth Pogue, who had lived in the house, moved to San José where she died in 1968.

Carmel Bay *by Maurice Del Mue, 1918. Del Mue was awarded a silver medal at the 1915 Panama-Pacific International Exposition in San Francisco. Peter Rohde also exhibited paintings at the Exposition. Courtesy Harvel L. Jones,* Twilight and Reverie: California Tonalist Painting 1890-1930. *Oakland, Ca: The Oakland Musuem, 1995.*

THE ROHDE FAMILY

Peter Hansen Rohde was born in Odense, Denmark, in 1879. Peter's family later moved to Neustadt in the Schleswig-Holstein area, where the Germans threatened to take control from the Danes. His father did not want his sons to be subject to conscription in the German army, so Peter's father said, "We're going to America!" The family gathered their belongings, sold everything they could not take with them, and took passage by ship to the United States.

The family landed at Ellis Island, New York as a part of the great immigrant stream. The family proceeded to California, arriving in 1893. Several of Peter's brothers and sisters, including Chris and Jens, became ranchers in the area of Modesto, Ceres and Turlock in California. Hans became a merchant seaman on Danish ships sailing between San Francisco and Alaska, taking lumber north and bringing back cod and salmon. Another brother, Neils, was the first member of the family to come to Santa Clara, where he worked as a cooper making barrels. Subsequently he went to the Maricopa oil fields and then to Columbia where he worked as a prospector and miner for the rest of his life.

Another brother, Arendt, born in Denmark in 1862, came to California with the family, where he and Peter became master housepainters in San Francisco. While painting houses to earn a living, both became interested in the fine arts. Arendt worked in oil, painting landscapes, Chinatown scenes and other subjects in a representational style. Arendt married, and with his wife and family, moved to Burlingame. He later died in that city in 1942.

Peter met Mary Madsen who had been born in San Francisco. Her father was a Danish sea captain who was lost at sea. Her mother was financially unable to care for her children and gave Mary up for adoption to the Fledkjer family in San Francisco. She and Peter were married and had three children, all born in the family home on 21st Street in San Francisco's Mission District.

The children were Claude born in 1907, Walter born in 1913, and Stanis born in 1914.

Peter developed a studio in the back of his San Francisco home. He became an active member of a well-known group of Bay Area artists who flourished from the turn of the century for several decades. Peter studied art at several art schools, including the Mark Hopkins Institute of Art, and with Gottardo Piazzoni and Ralph Stackpole at the California School of Fine Arts. He developed facility in the use of oils, etching, sculpturing and glass plate photography. Peter became especially noted as a still-life, portrait and landscape painter and etcher. He maintained friendships with noted artists of the day like Xavier Martinez, Carl Oscar Borg, Armin Hansen, Julia Heyneman, Gottardo Piazzoni, Joseph Raphael, Clarence Hinkle, Maynard Dixon and Arthur Putnam.

Piazzoni had a ranch in Carmel Valley which he and Peter Rohde enjoyed visiting from time to time, painting and sketching the area. One time, Piazzoni was engaged to paint murals at the San Francisco Public Library, but he needed a special large easel to do the work, so he borrowed Peter's. When the easel was returned, it was thickly covered with paints from the monumental project at the library!

Many of these artists belonged to the Bohemian Club and visited the studios of one another on the Montgomery block, discoursing on their work and occasionally exchanging paintings with one another. Hinkle did an exceptionally good oil portrait of Peter. Peter also did some portraits, including a very fine oil painting of his father and one of his wife's adoptive father. One of Peter's friends was an artist by the name of Maurice Del Mue whose sister married Gottardo Piazzoni.

Another of Peter's close friends was N. R. Helgesen, a well-known San Francisco art dealer who helped many artists of the day and provided appropriate gold leaf frames for their work. His gallery handled works by most of the noted artists and he, Piazzoni, and

Peter took a few camping and sketching trips together. When Peter moved to Santa Clara, Helgesen and his wife were frequent visitors to the Rohde home.

Ralph Stackpole was another noted artist of the time. Stackpole also had studied at the Mark Hopkins Institute of Art and later apprenticed himself to Arthur Putnam, the noted sculptor. After the 1906 earthquake and fire, Stackpole joined Putnam and Piazzoni in their studio in Paris. He returned to California in 1908 and achieved great renown for his painting and sculpture. Stackpole was a close friend of Peter's and lived in a home on Telegraph Hill overlooking the bay. When the squarish style home needed to be painted, Stackpole called on his friend Peter to do the job. When Stackpole's wife had a baby, he and Peter went to the hospital to bring mother and child home. En route, Stackpole said, "I think I'll call him Peter." Peter Stackpole himself became a noted photographer, working for years with *Life* Magazine and taking many significant pictures related to the construction of the bridges over San Francisco Bay and the Golden Gate.

Peter participated in the annual exhibitions of the San Francisco Art Association and in 1912 became an American citizen. Peter exhibited two paintings in the Panama-Pacific Exposition in 1915 and with his brother Arendt showed paintings at the 1939 World's Fair on Treasure Island. Peter became a member of the Master Painters Association of San José and taught at San José Technical High School, showing students how to grain wood.

Finding the climate of San Francisco a difficult one for his family, Peter moved to a home on Lincoln Street in Santa Clara in the early 1920s. His children were students at the Fremont, Intermediate and High Schools. Later the family purchased two homes at the corner of Poplar and Main streets, one for a family residence and the other as a rental. They occupied the home until the Santa Clara School District purchased both properties for the construction of the Townsend Football Field of

Franklin Street, Santa Clara, California, circa 1900. Courtesy Post card collection, Stocklmeir Library/Archive, California History Center, De Anza College.

Santa Clara High School. As a part of the purchase, the ownership of the rental was reserved and it was moved to property purchased from Pacific Manufacturing Company on Alviso Street.

After graduation from Santa Clara High School, Walter, Claude and Stanis formed a contract painting business with their father, Peter, called Peter Rohde & Sons. Painting, graining and decorating were the specialties of the firm, which did work from San Francisco to Monterey, including some of the mansions in Hillsborough and Atherton. Many of the homes built by Peter Pasetta in the Santa Clara area were painted by the firm.

When Peter Pasetta built his own home on Park Avenue in Santa Clara, Pasetta asked Peter Rhode to do the painting and in particular asked him if he could give the beams in the living room the appearance of being old and weather-beaten. Peter said, "Sure I can do that," and proceeded to do the work. About two weeks after the job was finished, Pasetta told Peter that he wanted to see him. Taking Peter into the living room, Pasetta pointed to the gable of the beamed ceiling and asked, "What do you see up there?" Peter responded, "I see some cobwebs." Pasetta slapped him on the back and said, "You know, Pete, you even fooled the spiders with your antiquing work!" In relating this story to his family, Peter commented that Pasetta was a good man, "but he has a sharp pencil!"

During the Depression, the Santa Clara Public Schools obtained financial assistance for a beautification project through the federal Works Progress Administration. At the suggestion of Emil Buchser, Peter Rohde was engaged to supervise the painting of all of the schools in Santa Clara. This project provided welcomed employment for many painters and resulted in the beautification of the school buildings.

Peter's son Claude served in the U.S. Air Force during World War II with the 450th Bomb Group as a technical sergeant, lab chief of the photography section of his group serving in the Italian theater. Upon leaving the service, Claude attended the California School of Fine Arts in San Francisco under the G.I. Bill where he pursued photography studying under Ansel Adams and Minor White.

Walter became a journeyman painter, carpenter and millman, working for a time at Pacific Manufacturing Company and for 19 years for Crest Cabinet Company in Santa Clara. During World War II, he worked at the Permanente Magnesium Defense Plant and also served in the California State Guard, achieving the rank of technical sergeant. Encouraged by his father's success, Walter studied art with Helen Dooley, Farmer Cook, and Mandelawitz, becoming adept in watercolor and photography. Walter was also involved in the formation of the San José Art League, which was headed by Fred Kessler, and was active in local camera clubs, showing his work in the Santa Clara County Fair and at local galleries.

Stanis also worked as a house painter and served as a construction machine operator with the 817th Engineer Aviation Battalion during World War II in Algeria, Tunisia, Sicily, Naples, Foggia, Rome and Arno. He later was employed by the Santa Clara School District as custodian and to paint school buildings.

Walter recalled his father discussing a job which had been given to his friend Piazzoni by the owner of Merner Lumber Company in Palo Alto. Piazzoni was to serve as an interior decorator stenciling and painting in pastel shades the beams of a large home being built in that city. Since Piazzoni was accustomed to work with smaller quantities of paint, he expressed concern about mixing the same colors in large quantities to apply to the beams in accordance with the stencils he had made. Piazzoni obtained Peter's assistance in producing large amounts of the paints in the exact colors which Piazzoni had mixed on the palette.

On one occasion, while doing his own decorating job for a residence, Peter was graining an imitation mahogany panel on the living room door. The owner, who was an old lady, was watching the operation from behind him. As Peter grained the door panel, he twirled his brush around to create the appearance of a knot, and then tapped the knot with his knuckle to lighten its center. The owner asked, "Why don't you make the knot bigger?" Peter replied with a smile, "I don't want to make them any bigger because they might fall out."

Both Peter and his wife died in Santa Clara and are buried with their son, Claude, in the veterans' section of the Santa Clara cemetery. Walter, a bachelor, and Stanis, a widower, lived in the family home filled with memories of the days when their father was a part of the Bay Area art scene.

Peter Hansen Rohde and his wife Mary were competent hardworking people who appreciated the opportunity available to them in California and in Santa Clara. They were devoted to their children, instilling in them high principles, important skills and a spirit of creativeness. These values and contributions form an important part of the Santa Clara saga.

THE KULPA FAMILY

John Kulpa and Airi Lehto Kulpa are two first generation Santa Clarans who contributed much to the city's development. Airi Lehto was born in Mayger, Oregon, in 1916. Her father, Nestor Lehto, immigrated from Finland in 1904 at age 20. He was a dairy farmer and raised row crops and from time to time he also worked as a fisherman. Her mother, Lizzie Lydia Salmon, was from South Dakota, descended from a Finnish family. Airi's parents married in Oregon and had eight children, five of whom survived, Edna, Elma, Ruben, Airi and Reino. Airi was named for her sister who drowned in an unfortunate accident when the sis-

The Kulpa home covered in snow after an unusual snowfall in the early 1960s. Courtesy Kulpa family to the Austen Warburton Collection.

Airi Kulpa and her children John and Katharine in a blossoming Santa Clara orchard, 1961. The orchard was replaced by the San Tomas Woods subdivision. Courtesy Kulpa family to the Austen Warburton Collection.

ter was only 18 months of age.

Airi married Allen Andrade, an Air Force officer during World War II, but the marriage ended in divorce. Airi took up newspaper work with the *Mexico City Herald* and other papers, and she was persuaded to join the public relations office of Twentieth Century-Fox West Coast Theaters. She married again in 1949 and became a full-time mother to her two children: John, born in 1950, and Katharine in 1952. This marriage also ended in divorce in 1956.

Meanwhile, John Kulpa was employed in Hartford, Connecticut, by United Aircraft Corporation, specializing in photography for special research projects. John and Airi met at a photographic convention in Los Angeles, and they were married in 1959. Since John was employed in Sunnyvale, the couple decided to find a home in the Santa Clara area, and they became the first family to move into the Forest Park development, establishing their new home at 487 Luther Drive. The Kulpas pursued their longtime interest in gardening and developed a beautiful and extensive garden which attracted flower enthusiasts, garden clubs and students alike.

As the children, John and Katharine grew, the family became active with school affairs, scouting and "Sailorettes," participating in as many as 24 parades in one year!

Aerial view of Forest Park Subdivision taken by John Kulpa, 1960. The street that runs from the top to the bottom of the photo is Pruneridge Avenue which ran through a prune orchard. The large thoroughfare at the bottom of the photo is Kiely Boulevard. Courtesy Kulpa family to the Austen Warburton Collection.

Airi Andrade (first husband's name) [Kulpa] center, with Sid Grauman of Grauman's Chinese Theatre in Hollywood (left) and Charles P. Skouras, head of Twentieth Century Fox Studios, 1948. Airi worked for Twentieth Century in their public relations department until 1950. Courtesy Kulpa family to the Austen Warburton Collection.

At about the same time, Airi attended a meeting at Villa Montalvo in Saratoga where a woman inquired where Airi lived. When Airi told her Santa Clara, the woman walked away "with her nose in the air." Airi was both shaken and angered at this attitude toward her home city and decided to devote her time to help build the image of the community. She offered her public relations talent to the new library, the building of the downtown, serving on the city's Citizens Advisory Committee, and supporting worthy candidates for public office. She recognized the need for appropriate press coverage and wrote many articles for local newspapers. She and John, both talented photographers, attended many events taking photographs and ensuring that the coverage of the events was accurate and appropriate.

Airi wanted to honor people who had made beneficial contributions to Santa Clara and instituted recognition programs and the Santa Clara Heritage Committee. Airi and Austen Warburton also persuaded the city to adopt the Sister Cities program, and Coimbra, the ancient capital of Portugal, was chosen as Santa Clara's first Sister City.

Mary Warburton, a charter member of the Santa Clara Woman's Club, visited the Kulpa home along with Ann Talia, another active member in the Woman's Club and garden enthusiast. Mrs. Warburton and Mrs. Talia encouraged Airi to join the Woman's Club and sponsored her admission. Thereafter Airi did extensive press coverage for the many activities of the club and it won state recognition for its accomplishments.

Airi also was active with the Triton Guild, the Historic Landmarks Commission, the Santa Clara Cultural Society, the Philharmonic Auxiliary, Gardeners Anonymous, and the Camellia Society. She assisted with public relations and publicity for many organizations as well as the Santa Clara community. She encouraged parties for recognition of authors who were residents of Santa Clara, helped the Friends of the Library, and authored a column for the *Santa Clara American*. Airi was honored by the Santa Clara Chamber of Commerce as Santa Clara's Woman Volunteer of the Year in 1968.

After 38 years of employment with UTC, John Kulpa retired in 1976 and the couple built a lovely home overlooking the ocean in Shelter Cove, California. Their garden blossomed profusely and attracted garden enthusiasts from throughout the state and foreign countries. Although John and Airi Kulpa moved to Shelter Cove, they retained a keen interest in Santa Clara and were recognized by the community for their contributions to the Santa Clara saga.

Santa Clara's first sister city was Coimbra, Portugal. The one-time capital of Portugal is located about 150 to the north of Lisbon and has a lot in common with Santa Clara. For one thing, it is home to a Jesuit university. It also has a convent, not unlike Santa Clara's Carmelite Monastery, and it boasts a similar climate.

In 1972, visiting dignitaries from Coimbra included Professor Andre Da Silva Campos Neves and his wife Maria Theresa Campos Neves. A local celebration was held in their honor and it was hosted by the Santa Clara Citizens Advisory Committee, which included Airi Kulpa and Austen Warburton who had been instrumental in getting the sister cities program off the ground in Santa Clara.

INDEX

Page entries in bold face refer to illustrations.

A

Acme Saloon, 57
Acronico, C. , **16**
Adams, Ansel, 89
Agnew, 45
Aguilo, Pedro, 65
Alaska, 41, 43
Alemany, José, 4
Alien Enemy Hearing board, 61
Alta California, *see* California—Spanish period
Alviso, 22-24, **22**, **23**, 34
Alviso, Domingo, 24
Alviso, Juan Ygnacio, 24
Alviso, Maria Bernal , 24
Alviso, Maria Pacheco , 24
Amaral Mechanical Co., 47
Amaral Plumbing, 47
Andrade, John, 66
Anza expedition, 24
Applegaith, Mrs., 85
Arbuckle, Clyde, 40
Arcane family, 22
Arguello family, 13, 17
Arguello, José, 18
Association of Friends of Junípero Serra, 65
Augustin, Raphael, 10
Auzerais, Edward, 13

B

Bacigalupi, James, 57
Bacon Ford Agency, 45
Baja California, 6, 10

Bank of America, 13, 19, 29
Bank of Italy, 13, 18
Bank of Santa Clara County, 31
Bank robberies, 48
Barcells, Frank J., 65
Barr, James, 34
Bauza-Roca, Antonio, 65
Belick, A. S., **44**
Bellarmine College Preparatory, 19
Ben Fernish Drugstore, 25
Bennett family, 22
Berry, Miss, 86
Bicentennial celebration 1976 , 75
Big Sur, 7
Bill Wilson Center, 30
Binder, Earle, 34
Bishop, Soreno, 82
Blake's Pharmacy, 27
Blake, Les, 56
Block Packing Company, 38, 58
Blue and White Grocery
     see Red and White Grocery
Bogardes, J., **33**
Bohannan, David D., 86
Bojorquez, Maria, 10
Bracher Ranch, 58
Breitweiser Baking Company, 28
Brier, W. J., 22-23
Broncos, *see* Santa Clara University—
     Football team
Brother Juniper, 5

Brotherhood of Railroad Trainmen,
     see United Transportation Union
Brothers, Henry, **33**
Brown family, 63
Brown, Edmund, 61
Buchser, Emil, 69, 70, 86
Buchser, Rudy, **85**
Buchte, Bruce, 19
Bull Moose Party, 36
Bull, Carolina, 81
Bull, Frederick, 81
Burnett, David M., 14
Burnett, John, 27
Burnett, Peter, 14
Butcher family, 76
Butcher's Corner, 76

C

Cajon Pass, 23
Calabasas Creek, 3
California
     Mexican period, 13
     Spanish period, 3-13
     Spanish settlements of Alta California, **11**
California Cherry festival, 24-25
California History Center, 1
California Pioneers of
     Santa Clara County, 38, 40
California State Legislature, 31-32
Callejon, Antonio, 72
Callejon, Catherine, 72